Active Parenting Of Teens
Parent's Guide

By Michael H. Popkin, Ph.D.

Published by Active Parenting, Inc., Atlanta Georgia
Copyright © 1990 by Active Parenting, Inc. All rights reserved.
Printed in the United States of America

ISBN 0-9618020-3-0

To the memory of

Bernard Howard

(1916 to 1989)

There are those who throw bricks through the dreams of others, and those who provide bricks for others to build their dreams. Bernie Howard was a dream builder. Whenever someone came to him with an earnest dream that could help others, his position was always, "How can I help?" Whether it was providing dignified care for the elderly, shelter for the homeless or a new approach to parent education, Bernie Howard reached for his checkbook when others reached for the door. When his advice was needed for writing a business plan or planning a building project, he was never too busy. He was there.

His contribution to the founding of Active Parenting is remembered in this dedication. May his memory live as long as caring people continue to support those who care about children and teens.

Acknowledgement

Active Parenting of Teens, like its predecessor, The Active Parenting Discussion Program, is based largely on the work of Alfred Adler and Rudolf Dreikurs, two of the great psychological thinkers of the 21st century. Their principles and methods have proven effective for millions of parents and educators throughout the world, and we are grateful for their many contributions.

Also acknowledged is Thomas Gordon, whose Parent Effectiveness Training helped pave the way for many of the parent education programs that followed. The concepts of problem ownership and "I" Messages that appear in Active Parenting of Teens had their roots in Tom's pioneering work.

I am also pleased to acknowledge the influence of many fine teachers who helped prepare me over the years to write this program, especially Kenneth Matheny and Roy Kern of Georgia State University; Oscar Christensen of the University of Arizona; and Frank Walton of Columbia, South Carolina.

To the hundreds of teenagers whom I worked with over the years as a camp director, and later as a therapist, and to their parents, thank you for the opportunity to have learned along with you. The experience has enriched this program.

A special thanks goes to the many Active Parenting leaders who over the years have made the original Active Parenting Discussion Program a huge success. You have given us the encouragement and wherewithal to develop Active Parenting of Teens. We will continue to listen to you as you share your needs and the needs of the parents you serve.

To those of you who read the original manuscripts and video scripts for this program: Melanie Bankhead, Mobile, AL; Sandy Barclay, Fayetteville, AR; Kenwyn Hopper, Lake Forest, IL; Juanita Johnson, Norwich, NY; Jane Oczkewicz, Port Orchard, WA; Susan Reed, Sioux Falls, SD; and Marilyn Ternay, Arlington, TX. Thank you for your excellent feedback. You have helped to make this a better program.

Thanks also to the staff of Active Parenting Publishers for putting me in quarantine every morning so that I could complete this program on schedule. Your support and enthusiasm for our work make it a pleasure to come in to work every day. To Susan Greathead, our director of program development, thank you for your many fine ideas about the content of this program, and for continuing to demand the highest standards in the development of materials.

I also express thanks to our two editors, Susan Palmer, for her fine work on the Parent's Guide, and Susan Halloran, for adding her expertise to the video script. (It seems that this project has been graced with a trio of Susans!)

Finally, thank you to my wife, Melody, and daughter, Megan, for your support at home, especially during those times when I was hard at work at the computer. You make it a pleasure to do my homework.

Photography by Dail White

Preface

"We are all here because we are scared to death about what our children will do when they become teenagers." These words, spoken by a father in a parenting group that I led over 15 years ago, still echo in my ears. Here we were dealing with parenting issues that related to their 5-year-olds and the parents' motivations for being there was fear of the teen years.

And why not? The difficulties in raising young children can escalate into life-and-death issues during the teen years. The statistics on teen drug use, pregnancy, delinquency, and even suicide are enough to give any concerned parent pause for reflection. Am I doing all that I can to prepare my teen to face these challenges? Although we can never guarantee our children's success, we want to know in our hearts that we have given them our best.

Part of giving our best means tackling the job of parenting like we would any other job that is both important AND difficult. This means getting the training and support that will help us parent effectively. For too long, our society has treated parenting as if it were either unimportant or easy, and left parents to fend for themselves. The frustration and conflict that resulted from this type of seat-of-the-pants parenting left many families wondering, what went wrong? Why weren't their teenagers growing up like Bud and Princess on "Father Knows Best," or like those wholesome Nelson boy on "Ozzie and Harriet"? Parenting is a lot harder than it seemed to be on those old sitcoms. In fact, the news that Ricky Nelson in real life had to combat a serious cocaine problem confirms that the risks are real and the solutions not easy.

Fortunately, there are answers. We have learned a lot over the years about what works and what doesn't work with teenagers. In addition, more and more of the institutions and professionals that serve families have committed themselves to offering parent education programs such as Active Parenting.

They are supporting you in the essential work of parenting, and in doing so are making a real contribution to your family and community. We hope that you will support their efforts by telling other parents about them.

Finally, a word about the other parents in your Active Parenting of Teens group. They, and your group leader, offer you a wonderful resource for applying the information and skills in this book. My hope is that you will support each other, learn from each other, and eventually form parenting networks in your community. When parents band together to solve problems, communities flourish.

Please keep in mind as your progress through this program that you are the leader in your family, and that this program is a resource for you to use. Some of what you will read and see may not fit with your view of the world. I hope that you will keep an open mind and consider these ideas fairly, but in the final analysis you are the authority in your family, not I nor any other expert. Feel free to pick and choose from this program what feels right to you, or as one of our leaders so aptly put it, "I use the best and let go of the rest."

Here's to giving it your best!

Michael H. Popkin

Contents

Session

I

The

Active

Parent

Chapter 1

The Times
of Change

There is a joke about a teenager who was working in a small grocery store. A man came in one day and asked for half a head of lettuce. The teen, thinking to himself that this was as dumb a request as he had ever heard, told the man that he'd go to the back and check with the manager. Upon finding the manager, the teen proceeded to say, "There is some fool up front who wants to buy *half* a head of lettuce." As he spoke, he noticed out of the corner of his eye that the customer had followed him. Without missing a beat, the teen added, pointing to the customer, "And this fine gentleman would like the other half."

Teenagers. The word itself can produce mixed feelings of hope and anxiety in the calmest of parents. And why not? Like the young man in the above story, most teens seem to be able to move through a range of emotions and behaviors with dizzying speed. One moment sarcastic and hurtful, the next intelligent and witty. At times even cooperative. Sometimes a scared child, sometimes a competent young adult. Teens, it would seem, are chameleons, capable of anything...except consistency.

A Time of Change

Physically, emotionally, psychologically, intellectually, socially, you name it, and your teenagers are probably changing, and changing fast. This is a time of intense personal growth for them and a time of challenge for us as parents. Guiding our children through the teen years can be the most difficult of all the parenting tasks. The stakes are enormous. Over 500,000 teens attempt suicide each year. Fortunately, many more make a successful passage into adulthood and become responsible, happy citizens.

Dick Van Pattern, Active Parenting of Teens *narrator.*

Although we as parents cannot control this outcome, we do make a difference. We are not the only influence on our teenagers' development, but we are the influence that we can do the most about.

Psychologically, when people are undergoing intense change and the uncertainty that goes with it, they are the most open to outside influence. Society is full of influences — some good, some bad, some downright disastrous. Parents have the opportunity and responsibility to become the most positive influence in their teens' lives. This program is designed to provide you with the tools and understanding that will best enable you to fulfill this responsibility and lead your teenager towards successful adulthood.

Why "Active Parenting"?

During this program you will be exploring an "active" approach to parenting. On the other hand, many parents use what we might call a "reactive" approach. That is, they wait until their teen pushes them to their limit, and then *react*. Because of their frustration and anger, they often react with random discipline...or as one mother put it, "the screech and hit" school of parenting.

When parents react rather than act, they are allowing the teen to control the situation, as well as the parents' emotions. Problems tend to continue, or even get worse, as parents and teens replay the same painful situations over and over.

Our philosophy in *Active Parenting of Teens* is that it is the job of the parent, rather than the teen, to play the leadership role in the family. Leadership, however, is not a simple matter of laying down the law. Effective leadership in parenting, like effective management in business, depends on a combination of attitudes and skills. This program will help you develop both, so that you can better lead your teens into responsible adulthood.

This course is "active" in another sense: it uses learning methods which call for involvement on the part of all participants. Active learning is effective learning, and we believe we have developed an Active Parenting program which uses the most effective teaching approaches available. First, we will use the combined power of video presentations and group interaction; we think that you can become involved *actively* in such a process — that you can absorb information, sharpen your insights, hone your ideas, and share them with others. Second, we will have fun with group learning exercises in which every participant can take an active role. And third, we will make use of the information and activities included in this *Parent's Guide*.

A word of caution: In this class you will learn a practical model for understanding teenagers. This model, based on the work of Alfred Adler and Rudolf Dreikurs, and added to by others, has been used effectively by over a million parents, counselors, teachers and psychologists. It works.

However, it is put into use by human beings, and human beings, as we all know,

are imperfect. We make mistakes. During this course you will probably become aware of two kinds of mistakes:

- **First,** you will make mistakes as you learn these new skills. Mistakes are part of the learning process, and everyone makes them when trying out new skills. It is important that you accept your mistakes without punishing yourself for being imperfect. If you are too hard on yourself, you not only make yourself feel bad, you also put limits on your learning. This is because when we feel criticized, even by ourselves, we become defensive. Soon we don't even admit our mistakes to ourselves, and we lose the valuable opportunity to correct and improve our performance. Mistakes are for learning; please be gentle with yourself!

- **Second,** you may realize or recall mistakes that your parents made in your own family in the past. Almost everyone does. It is important that you recognize these mistakes, but it is much more important that you let them go. They are in the past, and though you can learn from them, it is useless to dwell on them now. How much better it is to concentrate on being the most effective parent that you can be!

Parents in Today's Society

Parenting, though still one of the most underrated jobs in our society, is now beginning to attract some of the attention and consideration it deserves. After all, if the future of our society is our children, then the key to that future rests primarily with parents and teachers. More and more schools, churches and synagogues, mental health centers and other community organizations are responding to this reality by offering support to parents through programs such as Active Parenting.

If the future of our society is our children, then the key to that future rests primarily with parents and teachers.

Yet, in many ways parenting is harder than ever. Do I work outside the home or stay home? Do I take a second job? Do I go back to school? How can I get some time just for me? How safe is that party she wants to go to? Is he using drugs? I wonder if they've had sex with anyone...what about AIDS?

Some of these questions have been around for years, but others are particular to this generation of parents.

The Purpose of Parenting

The basic purpose of parenting has not changed. We can state it like this:

The purpose of parenting is to protect and prepare our children to survive and to thrive in the kind of society in which they live.

Although this purpose has not changed over the years, the society in which we are living has. For one thing, it has grown more dangerous. While our parents worried that we might try beer or marijuana, today's teens not only find alcohol routinely served at private parties, but are being tempted with cocaine, crack and a host of other deadly and addictive drugs. Violent crime among and against teens is much higher today, and as we are all aware, even sex can now be life-threatening.

The job of parenting is to work yourself out of a job!

This poses special problems for you as the parent of a teen. Regarding our purpose as parents, we want to help *protect* our teens so that they will *survive*. Yet if we overprotect them (that is, not allow reasonable risk taking), we are not *preparing* them to *thrive* on their own. Keep in mind that the job of parenting is to work yourself out of a job! This means preparing your teen for independence. Three things will help:

1. Talk to other adults and teens to get an idea of what risks are reasonable in *your* community.

2. Develop an ongoing support group with other parents of teens. Teenagers have tremendous support groups among themselves, some of which lead them in destructive directions. To counterbalance this influence, parents must also learn to band together in support groups.

3. Allow your teen to develop independence *gradually*. Use your research on "reasonable risks" to guide you as you allow your teen more freedom, and

use your support group to back you up when setting limits on your teen's freedom. (We will discuss this concept in Session III.)

A Society of Equals

If the bad news about modern society is that it has become more dangerous, the good news is that it has also become more just. We can be proud that our country was founded on the principle that all people are created equal.

Unfortunately, the word "all" in 1776 seemed to mean only white men who owned land. The rest couldn't even vote. But the ball of social progress was moving, and during the next 150 years such milestones as the end of slavery, the beginning of the labor movement, and women's right to vote showed that we intended to fulfill the promise of democracy. Then, in the 1950s, with the advent of television, the movement for social equality took a giant leap forward. When Martin Luther King, Jr., spoke of his dream of equality for all humankind, the television cameras carried his message throughout the world. One group after another — blacks, Native Americans, Chicanos, students, women — began to demand that they too be treated as equals. Today, no group is willing to be treated as inferior, to unquestionably do what they are told, to speak only when spoken to, or otherwise allow themselves to be treated disrespectfully.

The Role of the Authority in a Society of Equals

Even in a society of equals, authorities still exist. The president in a corporation, the police officer on the beat, the principal in the school are examples of people who have the authority to make final decisions in their domains, and the responsibility to enforce those decisions. They are the leaders. However, it's not much use being a leader if no one is willing to follow you. Here then is an important principle of leadership:

Leaders get their authority from those they lead.

The same is true for parents. We are the authorities in our families. But to be effective, we must have the cooperation of our children. Let's look at three types of leadership, and how effective each is likely to be in our current society.

1. The Autocratic Style

An autocrat is one who has absolute control, and the autocratic parent is all-powerful in directing the lives of his or her children. The parent is a dominating, authoritarian figure who uses reward and punishment as tools to enforce his or her orders. Teens are told what to do, how to do it, where to do it. There is little or no room for them to question, challenge or disagree. The autocratic method of parenting worked reasonably well in eras when inequality was normal in social interactions, but it works poorly in today's atmosphere of equality.

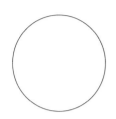

The autocratic style of parenting can be described as "limits without freedom," and depicted as a closed circle.

Children brought up in autocratic families seldom thrive. Either they have their spirits broken and give up, or, more often, they rebel. This rebellion usually happens during the teen years, because the child has developed enough power to fight back. Autocratic parenting has been the typical parenting style for so many generations that teenage rebellion has come to be accepted by many experts as "normal." This is a mistake. Teenagers, as we will see, do not have to rebel to become independent.

The autocratic style of parenting can be described as "limits without freedom," and depicted as a closed circle.

2. The Permissive Style

Permissive parents are those who are reacting strongly against the harsh and uncompromising autocratic method. Permissive parents allow their teens to "do their own thing." In such households, there is little respect for order and routine, and few limits are placed on anyone's freedom. Many such parents behave like rugs, allowing their teens to walk all over them. One of the main drawbacks of this system is the feeling of insecurity which plagues teens raised in this manner; they have almost no sense of belonging, and, because they have not learned to cooperate, they are often difficult to live with.

The permissive method is described as "freedom without limits," and shown as a squiggly line, meaning freedom run rampant.

Teens with permissive parents are often pampered and accustomed to getting their own way. When someone outside the family finally informs them that rules apply to them also, these teenagers often rebel. It is difficult to get a teenager who is used to a lifestyle with no limits to voluntarily begin obeying rules.

The permissive method is described as "freedom without limits," and shown as a squiggly line, meaning freedom run rampant.

3. The Active Style

The active parenting style is, in some respects, the middle ground between the autocratic method and permissive method, but it is also much more. In an active household, freedom is an ideal, but so are the rights of others and the responsibilities of all. The parent is the leader who encourages cooperation and stimulates learning. There is order and routine, and every person is an important member of the family.

The active style is described as "freedom within limits" and shown as a squiggly line within the limits of a circle.

In this program we will be exploring this active method. It is this method, in contrast to the other two, which acknowledges the social equality of the times in which we live, and which concentrates on the rights and responsibilities of all. The active method could be called "freedom within limits," and shown as a squiggly line within the limits of a circle.

In fact it could be shown as "freedom within *expanding* limits." As the child assumes more and more responsibility, the parent gradually relaxes the limits, until eventually the teenager has the same amount of independence as you or I.

Active Parenting acknowledges our democratic heritage and the role of social equality among all human beings in two important ways:

■ Teens, as well as parents, are to be treated with dignity and respect, even when the parents discipline them.

Democracy means you may not always get your way, but you always get your say.

■ Teens are entitled to express their thoughts and feelings, respectfully, to their parents. In this way they are given the right to influence the decisions that affect their lives. This is consistent with life in a democratic country, where you may not always get your way, but you always get your say.

The Fallacy of Reward and Punishment

We mentioned earlier that reward and punishment are tools which the autocratic parent uses to enforce his orders. Teens are kept in line by the threat of punishment if they misbehave, and the promise of reward if they do what the parent wishes them to do. This system of reward and punishment has been known to be effective in an autocratic environment, but in a society of equals, it doesn't work very well.

For one thing, a reward for good behavior comes to be expected almost as a right. If rewards are to be effective as incentives for continued good behavior,

---

the parent often must increase the value of the reward, until he reaches a kind of bankruptcy. This bankruptcy leads to the use of punishment.

Punishment is not effective in the long run because it often creates resentment on the part of the teen, and it leads him or her to find ways of getting even. In fact reward and punishment are out of place between equals. It is only a superior who can give rewards and mete out punishments, and it is only inferiors who can receive them. All in all, rewards and punishments, as methods of child-raising, are holdovers from an earlier time when the world was a different place. There are much more effective methods of discipline, and we will become acquainted with them in this program.

What Kind of Teen Do We Want to Raise?

Since the most important purpose of families has always been the survival of their members, and the teaching of survival skills to their children, it makes sense that the kind of teen we would want to raise is a teen who will survive in a democratic environment. And, to be complete, we would say not only "survive," but also "thrive." So what qualities are important for surviving and thriving in a democratic society? We think there are at least three:

- **Courage** is the first. Alfred Adler once said that if he could give one gift to a child, it would be courage. If a child were courageous, he reasoned, that child could learn everything else that he needed to learn. Coupled with parental guidance, a child's courage enables the child to try, to fail, and to try again, until he or she masters the challenges that life poses. With too little courage, the child gives up easily, or does not try at all. Fear that generates failure, and failure that reinforces fear become a network which supports a lifelong attitude of regret and resentment. Courage is a foundation upon which the teen constructs his or her personality. It is the heart of the human potential. In this course, we consider courage to be so essential to the teen's development that we devote the entire second part to methods of encouraging teenagers, and we will be referring to courage again and again.

Courage is a foundation upon which the teen constructs his or her personality.

- **Responsibility** is the second quality which teens need in order to thrive in a democracy. Rudolf Dreikurs, building on the foundation laid by Adler, stressed the importance of responsibility for individual growth and survival. A democracy demands that its members make decisions and accept responsibility for the consequences of those decisions. Without individual responsibility, our cherished freedoms will give way to govern-

Teens will be held responsible for their choices by experiencing the consequences that follow.

mental responsibility, where the state will gladly make decisions for us.

With freedom and choice comes the responsibility for the consequences of those choices. The reality of our society is that its teens will be called upon to make thousands of choices, and they will be held responsible for their choices by experiencing the consequences that follow. Some of these choices will be life-and-death matters. They will be offered drugs; will they choose to accept? They will face choices about drinking, sex, crime, dropping out, and even suicide. And their parents won't be there to tell them what to do. But if they have been prepared to make responsible decisions, and have instilled in them the courage to stand behind these decisions, then they will be prepared to meet these challenges. We will explore methods designed to teach responsibility to teens throughout the program and especially in Session III.

Cooperation from teens cannot be demanded; it must be won.

■ **Cooperation** is the third essential quality teens need to develop. In some circles a great deal of emphasis has been placed on competition as the road to success. In reality it has always been those individuals who have been aware of the magic of teamwork who have moved society forward. And so, helping a teen to learn that life is neither dependent nor independent, but rather an inter-dependent experience, is a cornerstone of Active Parenting. In a society of equals, cooperation skills have high value, and the teen who can cooperate with others in any enterprise is far more likely to survive and thrive than one who has never learned. The relationship of teens and parents is ideally one of coop-eration rather than conflict. But cooperation from teens cannot be demanded; it must be won. In each session we will focus on a particular method of achiev-ing cooperative relationships between parents and teens through "Family Enrichment Activities." In addition, Session IV is devoted to teaching ways of winning cooperation.

The goal of this program is to provide you with the information and skills that will enable you to raise courageous, responsible and cooperative young adults. These three qualities will be discussed frequently in these sessions, and they will be woven into every aspect of the program — the video presentations, the class discussions, the role plays, the assignments and the home activities.

As you learn, we urge you to stay aware of your own responsible, cooperative and courageous behavior.

Chapter 2

The Nature of the Beast (or Best?)

Today's accelerated modern society seems to bring out the beast in teenagers, rather than their best. It forces teenagers to grow up too fast. It panders to their need for challenge, in dangerous and destructive ways. (And worst of all, society does not need them to run effectively.)

All in all, society as we have created it is not a very positive place to raise teenagers. If we as parents are too permissive, the negative influences inherent in society will do our parenting for us. Yet if we are too autocratic, we are likely to drive our teenagers away from us, and into the same negative influences. It is only by taking an active approach to parenting that we can help guide our teens through the obstacle course of modern living, and prepare them to thrive.

Let's begin by considering how we can best influence our teens towards becoming responsible, courageous and cooperative citizens.

Purpose Not Cause

In order to understand another person's behavior, it does very little good to look back and try to figure out what *caused* the behavior. Human beings are not chemicals, and are not subject to the laws of cause and effect. We are beings with free will who *choose* how to behave based on our experience, values and goals for the future. So to understand why people, including teenagers, behave the way they do, we always want to ask ourselves, "What is their goal?"

Because many of our important goals and purposes operate at an unconscious level, it is often difficult to know what a person is up to. The same is true for our teens.

To understand why teenagers, behave the way they do, we can ask, "What is their goal?"

For example, 14-year-old Jason insists on wearing a pierced earring because all the other guys in his group are wearing them. His parents are furious, and absolutely forbid him to get his ear pierced. Jason does it anyway.

Why has Jason refused to comply with his parents' orders? What is his purpose or goal? To answer this question, we want to look at five basic goals of all teenage behavior, then see which Jason might achieve through his behavior.

Five Goals of Teen Behavior

Building on the foundation laid by the great psychologist, Rudolf Dreikurs, I suggest that there are five goals that govern teen behavior:

- Contact
- Power
- Protection
- Withdrawal
- Challenge

Let's look at each of these goals of human behavior more closely, particularly as it appears during the teen years.

1. Contact

The basic need of every human being is to belong.

The basic need of every human being is to belong. A baby could not survive without others to depend upon. Neither could the human species have survived throughout history without membership in various groups: families, communities, city states, nations, to name a few.

Out of this desire to belong, each of us develops the goal of making contact — physical or emotional — with other human beings. For an infant, the need to be held is actually critical to its survival. Later, contact with mom and dad helps the growing child develop a sense of belonging in the family. The self-esteem and courage that grow out of this belonging make it possible for the child to make positive contact outside the family. Schools, churches or synagogues, sports leagues and other institutions offer additional opportunities for contact and belonging.

Because the process of child development is a gradual move from the infant's total dependence on the parent towards the independence of the young adult, an interesting transition occurs during the teen years. Friends suddenly become more important than family. This is tough for many parents to accept. Why would he rather just "hang out" with the guys than go with us to the park? The answer is because he knows, at least unconsciously, that his future lies in moving *out* of the nest, and this is his testing ground. Certainly there is room for family activities in this process, but we need to understand that acceptance by his peers is now more critical than acceptance by his parents.

Example: Jason's desire to wear an earring may have been prompted by his goal of contact. If the other guys in his group were wearing a similar earring, he may have felt that it was more important to belong with his peers than with his family.

2. Power

Each of us wants to influence our environment and to gain some measure of control over it. We would like for things to go our way; we want the power to make that happen. As we learn how to use our power effectively, our self-esteem increases and we feel ourselves thriving.

Each of us wants to influence our environment and to gain some measure of control over it.

During the teen years, our goal of power becomes heightened. We have grown physically into more powerful beings who are now not only bigger and stronger, but capable of reproducing other human beings. We are intellectually more powerful, capable of considering "what might be" as opposed to "what is." We want to use these new skills in new ways, so we become social critics of everything (including mom and dad) and bask in the power our new intelligence gives us...to argue. In fact, we find ourselves arguing for arguing's sake, just to enjoy our increased ability.

Although frustrating to live with, these experiments in empowerment are an important part of the transition from dependence to independence. Remember, if your teen is to successfully leave you as a child, to return as an adult, he or she must have the power to do so.

Example: Most teens feel that they should have the power to dress and look as they would like. When Jason's parents forbade him to wear the earring, they challenged his sense of independence. He may have thought that to be powerful in his own life, it was important for him to wear the earring in spite of their objections.

3. Protection

To survive and to thrive, we must be able to protect ourselves and our families. Our instinctive desire to repel attacks — whether physical or psychological — has led to the development of elaborate systems of justice and defense.

"You don't have to be just like us; you just have to abide by certain rules."

During our teen years, when our personal identity is taking shape, we will go to great lengths to protect our sense of self. We want to define ourselves as our own person, independent of mom and dad. In fact, when counseling teenagers, I often tell them that one of the most courageous things they can do is to do what they really want to, when it's also what their parents want.

As parents, we do not want to force our teens to openly rebel against our values in order to protect their emerging identity. But we can let them make such statements in safe ways, through choice of music, clothing and hair style, for example. We can also accept their point of view as valid, even when we disagree. We can give them the message that, "You don't have to be just like us; you just have to abide by certain rules."

Example: Jason's goal in wearing the earring may have also served to protect his emerging identity. "I don't want to be just like you; I don't want to be your clone."

4. Withdrawal

Just as time-outs are essential in any sport, they are an important part of life. We need time to withdraw from the demands of people, jobs and roles — to regroup, to center ourselves again. The goal of withdrawal acts as a healthy counterbalance to the goal of contact, and, of course, there are times when it is wise to withdraw from danger.

The wisdom to know when it is best to withdraw from danger and when it is right to go ahead or take a stand is difficult to acquire. Experience can help. Teenagers, who are long on the desire to meet a challenge, but short on experience, are going to make some mistakes. They will go along with the group at times when they should have withdrawn. They will take some reckless risks. We all did some things as teenagers, and young adults (an extension of the teen years for many), that we should have withdrawn from. As parents, we can use the communication skills in Session IV to help our teens learn from these mistakes, and not compound the problem with punishments and humiliation.

Our teens will want to withdraw into their own space.

We can also recognize that our teens will want to withdraw into their own space (usually their room) more frequently than we need to. This is normal behavior for most teenagers. However, there are two exceptions that you should be aware of: 1) if you suspect drug or alcohol use; and 2) if your teen is depressed. Both teen suicide and drug and alcohol statistics are much too high in our society. Too much withdrawal can be a signal that one of these major problems exists, and that the parent should get involved.

Example: It is doubtful that Jason's earring accomplishes the goal of withdrawal. However, he may choose withdrawal later to think about his decision, and whether taking the stand against his parents is worth it.

5. Challenge

The first four goals begin in childhood, and continue throughout our lives. The goal of challenge, though present in children and adults, seems to be strongest during adolescence. In fact, many cultures have devised a traditional challenge to be performed by the teenager to mark the transition from child to adult.

The goal of challenge seems to be strongest during adolescence.

The desire for challenge, to test ourselves against some outside obstacle, is a way of measuring how well we are doing on our journey from dependence to independence. Are we ready to take our place as fully functioning beings? Challenges are a necessary part of the answer.

The most basic challenges are against nature. In the primitive aborigine culture of Australia, the teenager was sent on a "walkabout" in which he tested his ability to survive on his own in a hostile environment. Unfortunately, in our high-tech society, most teens do not get a chance to experience this kind of natural challenge, which is so valuable in building self-esteem.

Example: Wearing an earring invites criticism from authority figures, and may set up a challenge situation if the adults take the bait. By making a major issue over the earring, Jason's parents have now challenged his independence. It may be hard for him to give in, and still save face.

Positive and Negative Approaches to the Five Goals

Active Parenting holds the belief that there are no good or bad kids, only those who choose to pursue these five basic goals in either positive or negative ways. Teens with high self-esteem and courage will generally choose the positive approaches. Those with low self-esteem who are discouraged will more likely choose the negative approaches. The following chart provides some labels we can use to distinguish these approaches:

TEEN'S GOAL	POSITIVE APPROACH	NEGATIVE APPROACH
Contact	Contribution	Undue Attention Seeking
Power	Independence	Rebellion
Protection	Assertiveness Forgiveness	Revenge
Withdrawal	Centering	Undue Avoidance
Challenge	Skill Building Reasonable Risk Taking	Thrill Seeking

How to Determine a Teen's Goal

Because parents do not usually know the real goals behind teen misbehavior, we often take an action that makes the problem worse. In other words, our discipline actually gives the teen a pay-off in terms of achieving his or her basic goal. And if negative behavior works, why not continue to use it? After all, it's usually the easier approach.

The first step then is to determine what your teen really wants. Once we know the goal, we can help the teen towards the positive approach to getting it.

This requires some detective work on our part. There are two clues that will usually tell us the teen's goal:

- Our own feeling during a conflict: Are we annoyed, angry, hurt, helpless or afraid?
- The teen's response to our attempts at correcting the misbehavior.

The following chart is a guide for using this information:

IF WE FEEL...	AND THE TEEN'S RESPONSE TO CORRECTION IS...	THEN THE NEGATIVE APPROACH IS...	TO THE TEEN'S GOAL OF...
annoyed	stops, but starts again very soon	Undue Attention Seeking	Contact
angry	escalates misbehavior or gives in only to fight again another day	Rebellion	Power
hurt	continues to hurt us or escalates the misbehavior	Revenge	Protection
helpless	becomes passive; refuses to try	Undue Avoidance	Withdrawal
fearful	takes more reckless risks	Thrill Seeking	Challenge

Let's look more closely at each of the five negative approaches.

1. Undue Attention Seeking

The teen who seeks to make contact through undue attention seeking is operating with the mistaken belief that he or she must be the center of attention in order to belong. While young children will do things to get this attention from their parents, teens prefer the attention of peers. They may become class clowns or the ones who are constantly in trouble — anything to stay in the limelight.

While the peer group may encourage such misbehavior, adults usually feel *annoyed* or *irritated*. When confronted by an adult, the teen will usually stop the misbehavior...for a while, but then continue again soon. This makes sense when we consider that the teen's goal is contact, and that by confronting the teen we give him that contact. For a while this satisfies his desire for attention, but not for long.

How parents pay off the negative approach of undue attention seeking: We tend to remind, nag, coax, complain, give mini-lectures, scold, and otherwise stay in contact with the teen. This attention, added to the attention the misbehavior gets from the peer group, tends to reinforce the teen's mistaken idea that misbehavior is how he or she can best belong.

Break the pattern avoiding the pay-offs which keep the mistaken ideas alive.

What can parents do differently? The key to helping your teen shift from the negative approach to the positive with any of the five goals is to do the unexpected. We have to break the pattern that the teen has come to expect, avoiding the pay-offs which keep the mistaken ideas alive. In the case of undue attention seeking, we want to act more and talk less. The discipline that works best is either a brief confrontation through an "I" Message or a logical consequence. (These techniques will be presented in Session III.)

Discipline is only half the procedure for helping a teen change approaches. It is designed to limit the negative behavior. However, just as important, we also want to actively encourage the teen towards the positive approach. In the case of undue attention seeking, we want to help the teen achieve the recognition and contact that he or she wants by playing a useful role. We can help find meaningful ways for the teen to contribute to the group, while ignoring some of the unproductive attention getting behaviors. (More about encouragement in Session II.)

2. Rebellion

Of the five negative approaches, rebellion is the most common and creates the most distress in families and schools throughout the country. The teen who becomes discouraged trying to achieve his or her goal of power through useful means can easily find power in the negative approach of rebellion. We talked earlier about how either an autocratic or permissive discipline style tends to influence the teen towards rebellion.

The teen's mistaken belief with this approach is that the only way to achieve power is to control others, or at least to show others that he can't be controlled by them. This behavior can be very frustrating for parents and educators, and the typical feeling that clues us that we are engaged in a power struggle is our own *anger*. If we express this anger to the teen and join in the power struggle, the teen's usual response is to intensify the struggle, and even escalate the misbehavior.

How parents pay off the negative approach of rebellion: There are two ways to lose a power struggle: 1) by fighting, and 2) by giving in. When we get angry and engage in a verbal fight, we are in effect saying to the teen, "Look how powerful you are; you have made me angry and pulled me down to your level." When we give in to a rebelling teen's unreasonable demands, we also give the message, "Look how powerful your rebellion is; it has gotten you your way."

The autocratic parent tends to err on the side of fighting. We think that we have the right to run our teens' lives. We pamper them by getting them up for school; we tell them what they may or may not wear, who their friends may be, how much to study, when to go to bed...the list goes on and on. Soon the teen decides that since he has no legitimate power, the only way to prove that "I run my own life" is to rebel. This rebellion may be active, in which case he will openly oppose adults, both at home and at school, wherever he perceives himself as being treated *To successfully side-* disrespectfully. Or his rebellion may be passive. A lack of motivation or apathy *step the struggle for* in many students is simply non-violent rebellion. It's as if the teen is saying, *power, we must refuse* "OK, you can make me sit here, but you can't make me learn; I still control my *to fight or to give in.* mind!" Either way, a power struggle is apparent.

The permissive parent, as well as the neglectful parent, tends to err on the side of giving in. This parent will do anything to avoid a confrontation, and so spoils the teen into thinking that everything should go his or her way. When life does not go their way, such teenagers demonstrate a short fuse and lack of perseverance. They have no skills for working out problems, nor the tolerance for accepting the rights and wants of others.

What can parents do differently? To successfully side-step the struggle for power, we must refuse to fight or to give in. The

Chapter 2 - The Nature of the Beast (or Best?)

autocratic parent can communicate more confidence in the teen's ability to make decisions by himself. We can let the teen make some mistakes, and then experience the consequences...without our lecturing or humiliating. We can set up family council meetings (Session IV) to involve the teen in making decisions that affect the whole family. We can use the family enrichment activities, communication skills, and methods of encouragement described in this program to begin winning a more cooperative relationship. And, most important, we can show the teen that we are not interested in fighting. Instead, we will work together to find solutions, and when discipline is necessary, we will use logical consequences (Session III) rather than anger and punishment.

The permissive parent, in addition to using the Active Parenting skills just described, can refuse to give in to the teen's unreasonable demands. We can stop being short-order cooks, clean-up services, wake-up callers, and last minute chauffeurs, and otherwise pampering our teens. We can set firm limits, negotiate within those limits, refuse to be intimidated by the inevitable display of anger, and enforce the consequences of breaking those limits (Session III). We can let our teens know that while we believe that they should be treated respectfully, we, in turn, expect them to treat us with respect.

3. Revenge

An escalation of the power struggle usually leads to the negative approach of revenge, especially if the teen feels that the parent has "won too many battles" or has hurt the teen in the process. The teen decides that the best form of protection is to hurt back. The parent's typical feeling is *hurt*, and because our autocratic tradition tells us that when teens hurt us, we should punish them more, an escalating revenge cycle begins.

Because parents want to see their teens survive and thrive, we can never win this revenge war. All the teen has to do to hurt us is fail. They can fail at school; they can fail with peers; they can fail with drugs, with sex, and, ultimately, they can fail at life by committing suicide. The result each time is a parent left hurting.

How parents pay off the negative approach of revenge: When teens seek to protect themselves by getting revenge, they are usually very discouraged with themselves. When we retaliate with punishment and put-downs, we both discourage them further, and confirm their belief that they have a right to hurt us back. The more we hurt them, the more they want to hurt us back.

What can parents do differently? Someone has to stop the revenge cycle if the situation is to improve. We can stubbornly demand that the teen change (which is what many of us have been taught to do), or we can play the leadership role in the family and call a cease-fire. By refusing to hurt back, we can do the unexpected and break the cycle.

By refusing to hurt back, we can do the unexpected and break the cycle.

It will help us to remember that no child is born "bad" or "mean." For teens to act this way, they have to be hurting inside. The first step, then, is to do what we can to stop whatever is hurting the teen. If it is *our* behavior, then we can take a new approach. If someone else is hurting her, we can support the teen in handling it herself, or take more direct action when appropriate. Sometimes, however, the teen has not been wronged, but is hurting because of her misconception about how life *ought* to work. Perhaps we have coddled the teen in the past, and now we have begun to treat the teen (and ourselves) more respectfully. In these cases a calm and firm manner will help. Finally, the skills discussed for handling a power struggle will also be useful in redirecting a revenge seeking teen.

4. Undue Avoidance

Teenagers who become extremely discouraged may sink so low in their own self-esteem that they give up trying. Their belief becomes, "I can't succeed so I'll avoid trying; then I can't fail." They develop an apathy and lack of motivation that often leaves parents and educators feeling helpless. Such teenagers may become truant from school, fail to do assignments, or even drop out. Alcohol and other drugs may become a way for these teens to avoid the challenges that life poses, and to find temporary relief from their own discouragement.

How parents pay off the negative approach of undue avoidance: It is often our own perfectionism that begins the teen's long slow slide into undue avoidance. When we focus excessively on mistakes, when nothing ever seems to be good enough for us, when all we talk about is his great "potential," the teen may give up trying altogether.

We can help the teen find tasks where she can succeed.

Once a teen has chosen avoidance, we often make the mistake of giving up on him. We write him off as a loser, and we stop making an effort to help. Or we yell and scream, humiliate and punish. Either way, we send the message that "You're not good enough for us." This confirms the teen's own evaluation of himself, and so justifies his avoidance.

What can parents do differently? We want to communicate to the teen that succeed or fail, win or lose, he or she is still our son or daughter, and we are

glad of it. Our love is unconditional. In addition to such acceptance of the teen, we will need to practice patience and give a lot of encouragement. We can remind ourselves that the teen is exaggerating her avoidance to see if the worst is true (that she is really as bad off as she thinks). We can help the teen find tasks where she can succeed, so that she can begin to break the misconception of herself as a loser. And we can help her to see that mistakes are for learning, and that failure is just a lesson on the road to success.

5. Thrill Seeking

When life seems dull and boring, and the opportunities for legitimate challenge and excitement are limited, the temptation is always there for destructive, thrill seeking adventure. Alcohol and drugs, sexual experimentation, reckless driving, and even breaking the law can be thrilling alternatives to a teen who sees everyday life as bland. For teens who are also choosing undue avoidance, thrill seeking may become the only thing they feel they are good at. "If I can't be the best student," the thinking sometimes goes, "then at least I can be the best druggie."

How parents pay off the negative approach to thrill seeking: When we are overprotective, and do not allow our teens to take any chances, we heighten the appeal of thrill seeking. Teens have a legitimate need to test themselves, and when we try to stifle such desire, it often becomes stronger. Another mistake that parents make is to react with anger and outrage when we find our teens using alcohol or engaging in other harmful thrill seeking behavior. This often turns the thrill seeking into a power struggle, so that the teen now has two motivations to continue: 1) the thrill; and 2) to show mom and dad that they can't run my life. (More on the critical issues of alcohol, drugs and sexuality in Sessions V and VI.)

We can help redirect the teen towards positive activities.

What can parents do differently? We can avoid turning this into a power struggle by remaining firm and calm. We can help redirect the teen towards positive activities such as karate; cycling; rock climbing; white water sports; team sports; a part-time job; hobbies such as mechanics, horses or computers; adventure organizations such as scouting or Outward Bound. We can help them enjoy vicarious thrills by taking them to ball games, and we can double the benefits by learning something together. (Haven't you always wanted to take karate lessons or learn automotive mechanics?) Of course, we do want to confront and discipline reckless behavior, and we will discuss this in detail later, but let's be more creative in our society by finding ways to help teens challenge themselves. This will eliminate much of the problem.

What About Out-of-Control Teens?

We have discussed that it is the parent's role in the family to be the leader, the authority. We've also said that one person cannot really *control* another person's behavior, that what we can do is *influence* him or her. We added to that the idea that an active style of leadership is more likely to influence our teens effectively than an autocratic or permissive style. And that...

Leaders get their authority from those they lead.

If you have used an autocratic or permissive approach for a long time, your teen may not acknowledge your legitimate right to be the authority in the family.

All teens will at one time or another break a rule, disobey their parents, or otherwise "get into trouble." When confronted by parents, these teens will accept that they were wrong and abide by the consequences the parent imposes. If you say they are not allowed to go out, they don't go out; if you say they may not watch TV until their grades come up, they may protest, but they accept that the final decision is yours. In other words they will allow you to control their behavior.

Teens who do not give up this control to their parents, who blatantly ignore their parents' decisions, who take the attitude "You can't stop me; I'll do what I want," and then do, are often called "out of control."

If you have a teen that is frequently out of control, you have experienced a lot of frustration. But the fact that you are taking this course means that you have not given up, and that you have the courage to look for help. Now, for some good news and some bad news. The good news is that things will change if you stick with it. The bad news is that it won't change overnight, and it may take more than this program to help you make it change.

There are three levels of help that you can pursue as needed:

■ **An Active Parenting of Teens group**
   The information and skills that you'll learn, coupled with the support of fellow parents, may be enough to help you win your teen back over. If not, add to this...

■ **Family counseling**
   Your leader or physician can recommend someone who specializes in

parent/teen problems. This person will build on what you are learning in this course, and will also directly involve your teen. If this isn't enough, the counselor can help you explore...

■ **In-patient treatment for your teen**
Some teens are so out of control that it takes a residential treatment facility such as a hospital or outdoor therapeutic program to help get them back within the limits.

The key is going to be your continued courage to stay with it, whatever it takes, until it gets better. Recognize that whatever mistakes you have made, you care (or you wouldn't be reading this); that means that given the necessary support, you've got what it takes to turn things around.

Filling Your Toolbox

There is an expression among people who build things about having "the right tools for the job." One of the problems with parenting in our society is that parents have been given the job, but not the tools. When confronted with a misbehaving teenager, if all you have in the bottom of your toolbox are a few worn out old punishments ("Okay, that's it; you're grounded!"), it's like trying to build a modern home with a rusty saw and a tack hammer.

This course is about skill building. Sure, I've covered a lot of theory in this first session because I wouldn't insult your intelligence by expecting you to do things without first explaining why they make sense. And I'll continue to give you the "whys." (Just as I hope that you will give your teens answers to their "whys," and not fall back on that old autocratic saw, "Because I'm the parent and I said so." How much better to be able to say, "Because this is the situation and this is what the situation calls for.")

Our goal is to put modern tools in your toolbox, so that you can build the best possible home for you and your family. In the sessions ahead we will cover a host of skills: encouragement skills, discipline skills, communication skills, problem solving skills, problem prevention skills, and family enrichment skills. We'll also look at special applications of these skills to the two biggest challenges facing all parents of teenagers: drugs and sexuality.

Whether your toolchest is nearly full or empty, by the time we are finished, you will have the skills you need to lead your teens towards responsible, cooperative and courageous behavior.

Family Enrichment Activity #1

"Taking Time for Fun"

Ever notice that a good salesperson will always spend time developing a positive relationship with you *before* he tries to sell you anything? He knows that half the job of effectively influencing a person is first developing that relationship. Once the person has been "won over," the sale is much easier. (Can you imagine a salesperson being autocratic and demanding a sale? "You'll buy this because I'm the salesperson and I said so!")

The same is true for parenting. The more you can enrich your relationship with your teen, the more influence he will allow you in his life. This will prevent many problems as well as make discipline much easier when it is called for.

In each session we will present a family enrichment activity for you to add to your toolchest. Use these, and the other support skills, to strengthen your relationship. If your teen is frequently out of control, this may be a way to begin making positive contact. Be creative. And reach out.

The first family enrichment activity is to take time to do something fun with your teen. It can be as brief as a few minutes, or as long as a day. The key is to make it fun. For example:

- Throw a ball or shoot baskets.
- Bake a fancy dessert.
- Play a game together.
- Roughhouse.
- Go on an outing, just the two of you.
- Go rafting down a river.

To get the most out of this activity:

- Find activities that you both enjoy.
- Ask for suggestions from your teen, but have some ideas of your own.
- Keep it fun! Do not use this time for confrontation.
- Record your experiences in your *Parent's Guide*.

Introduction

These are some things people often like sharing with each other at the beginning of the course:

Your name _____

Your partner's name (or write "single" if applicable)

_____

Your children's
names _____ age_____

_____ age_____

_____ age_____

Your work _____

One problem area for each teen that you'd like some help in solving:

1. _____

_____

_____

2. _____

_____

_____

3. _____

_____

_____

Please fill in each blank for your own benefit, but remember, throughout this program you need only share as much as you choose to share.

Identifying the Negative Approach

Write down a recent conflict that you had with one of your teens, including what happened, what you said, and what he or she did.

_____

_____

_____

How did you feel during the exchange? (irritated, angry, hurt, hopeless or afraid?)

_____

How did your teen respond to your attempts at correction?

_____

_____

Using the chart on page 26 of this *Parent's Guide*, what was your teen's negative approach? (undue attention seeking, rebellion, revenge, avoidance or thrill seeking?)

_____

What was the basic goal that your teen was after? (contact, power, protection, withdrawal or challenge?)

_____

What was one mistake that you made? In other words how did you pay off the negative approach to this goal?

_____

_____

_____

_____

Family Enrichment Activity #1

"Taking Time for Fun"

Remember When...

Remember something fun you enjoyed doing as a teenager with one of your parents. Close your eyes for a moment and visualize the pleasant experience.

What was the fun activity that you and your parent shared?

_____

How did you feel about your parent at that moment?

_____

How did you feel about yourself?

_____

Progress Chart

As you take time for fun with each of your teens, record the experience below:

Teen's name	What did you do?	How did it go?
	_____	_____
_____	_____	_____
	_____	_____
	_____	_____
_____	_____	_____
	_____	_____
_____	_____	_____
	_____	_____

Instilling
Courage and
Self-Esteem

Chapter 3

The Think-Feel-Do Cycle

A long time ago, before the advent of convenience stores, there was a race of humans called "milkmen." There was also a 5-year-old boy who was afraid of the dark. His mother, hoping to help him overcome his fear, encouraged the little boy to open the front door and bring in the milk. He was too afraid, but she persisted. "Go ahead," she said, "God is outside and He will protect you." The boy thought about that for a moment, then moved his tiny hand toward the door. He fearfully turned the knob to open the door, reached his little hand into that cold, black morning, and shouted, "If you're out there God, hand me the milk!"

Courage...One from the Heart

Preparing a child to courageously meet the challenges that life will certainly offer is perhaps the single most important aspect of Active Parenting. Courage is such an important quality in today's complex world of choices that it forms the very foundation upon which the child constructs his or her personality. From the French word "coeur," courage is the "heart" that enables us to take risks. And it is through risk taking that we are able to develop responsibility, cooperation, independence...and whatever else we may strive for. In fact we define courage in Active Parenting as:

The willingness to take a known risk for a known purpose.

Courage is a feeling. It is a feeling of confidence that allows us to take those risks. It is not the absence of fear, but the willingness to take a reasonable risk in spite of our fear. Without this feeling of courage, we often find ourselves sitting on the sidelines, unwilling to take the risks inherent in any endeavor. Without courage, we let life pass us by while we wishfully wait for someone else to "hand us the milk."

Self-Esteem...One from the Mind

Where does courage come from? It comes from a belief in ourselves. A belief that we are capable, lovable human beings who will eventually succeed. This belief in ourselves is commonly called "self-esteem." In other words we hold ourselves in high regard. When we think well of ourselves, when we like our chances to succeed, then it makes sense that we will have the courage to take risks. So...

High Self-Esteem　➡　Courage

Unfortunately, the opposite is also true. When we think poorly of ourselves, when we think we are not okay, that we are unlovable, not capable, then our self-esteem drops. This low self-esteem produces discouragement and fear.

Low Self-Esteem　➡　Discouragement

And when people of any age become discouraged, two things often happen: 1) They stop taking reasonable risks, so they stop developing; and 2) They become more likely to misbehave. We'll explore this connection between discouragement and misbehavior more in a moment, but first let's put all this together in a model for understanding human behavior.

The Think-Feel-Do Cycle

We have talked about the problems and opportunities that life poses. Let's call these "events." In other words, something happens. For example, your teenage daughter fails a chemistry exam.

EVENT (failed exam)

How do we respond to events in our lives? Since many events are emotionally charged, once they occur, we experience feelings. Here's where many people share a common misconception. They talk as if the events in their lives cause their feelings. For example, your teenage daughter may feel "depressed" about the exam. And you and she might both say that she feels depressed because she failed the exam. Or...

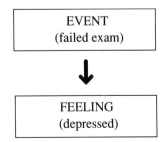

This is a mistake. The truth is that although other people and events do *influence* or *trigger* our feelings, the *cause* of our feelings — based on our beliefs, attitudes and values — is our thinking. Great thinkers have known this for centuries:

> Epictetus (the Greek philosopher): "Men are not disturbed by things, but by the view they take of things."

> Shakespeare: "There is nothing either good or bad, but thinking makes it so."

So, it isn't the failed exam that caused your daughter's depressed feeling in our example, but rather her thoughts about having failed the exam. What kind of thoughts might generate a feeling of depression? There are many. For example:

> *"I'm a failure."*
> *"I'm not capable."*
> *"My parents won't respect me anymore."*

Whatever the exact beliefs, we know by the strong feeling of depression that the teen in this example is thinking negative thoughts about herself. These thoughts lower her self-esteem, which makes her feel discouraged...

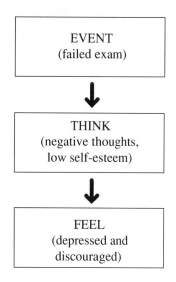

To complete our cycle, we need to add one final element: our behavior, what we *do* in response to an event. As you can probably guess from the model, what we do is a result of what we think and how we feel. When self-esteem is up and the teen feels a strong sense of courage, behavior is going to be positive. But when negative thinking leads to low self-esteem and discouragement, behavior is going to be negative.

What we *do* is particularly important because this is how we *influence* (Note: not control) the events in our life. If the teen is sufficiently discouraged, she might give up on school altogether (remember the negative approach of avoidance?). This behavior would lead to more failed exams, and probably to other negative events. This becomes a failure cycle.

Failure Cycle

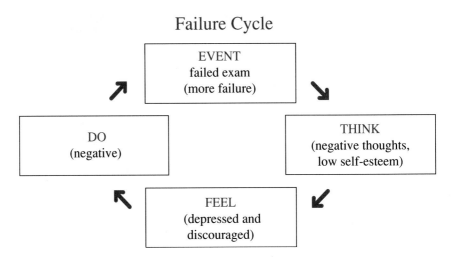

But let's say that the teen had high self-esteem and had been taught how to think rationally about setbacks and failure. Then her thinking might be much more positive:

> *"I guess I really blew this one. Let's see what I did wrong, so I don't mess up on the next one."*
> *"Failing doesn't make a person a failure, it just means she's got some more work to do."*
> *"Mom and Dad will love me whether I get As or Fs. I know I can count on that."*

With thinking like this, she may feel *disappointed,* but certainly not depressed or discouraged. Her positive thoughts have kept her self-esteem high and given her the courage to risk continuing the effort. Her plan to learn from the failure and *do* something about it will probably create positive events in the future. She is operating in a success cycle.

Since we want to see our teens in success cycles, it is important to learn how to help them achieve high self-esteem and courage.

Success Cycle

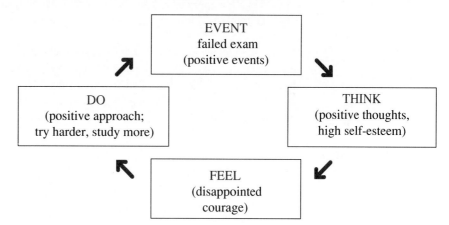

| EVENT |
| failed exam |
| (positive events) |

DO		THINK
(positive approach;		(positive thoughts,
try harder, study more)		high self-esteem)

| FEEL |
| (disappointed |
| courage) |

Since we want to see our teens in success cycles, it is important to learn how to help them achieve high self-esteem and courage. We'll look at specific methods of doing this in a moment. But first, let's recall the five basic goals of teen behavior that were discussed in Session I:

- Contact
- Power
- Protection
- Withdrawal
- Challenge

These goals fit into the Think-Feel-Do cycle under *think*, because our goals are part of our belief system. How teens approach these goals (that is, what they *do*), as we said in Session I, can be either positive or negative **depending on whether they FEEL encouraged or discouraged.** So, teens with high self-esteem feel encouraged and therefore approach their basic goals in positive ways. This usually produces positive results which trigger more positive thinking, and so on, in a "success cycle." In contrast, a teen with low self-esteem feels discouraged, and approaches the basic goals through a negative approach:

- Contact—undue attention seeking
- Power—rebellion
- Protection—revenge
- Withdrawal—undue avoidance
- Challenge—thrill seeking

These negative approaches usually produce negative results which trigger more negative thinking, more discouragement, and so on, in a "failure cycle."

What roles can we as parents and teachers play in these cycles? How can we influence our teens? Through our behavior, we become an *event* in the Think-Feel-Do cycle. What we say and do will influence our teen's thinking, which will in turn influence her feeling and behavior. (Of course, the teen's behavior then becomes an event in *our* lives, influencing us.)

The Paradox of Control

I have used the term "influence" rather than control for an important reason. Because people, and particularly teenage people, want very much to run their own lives (the goal of power), an interesting paradox occurs:

The more you try to control a teen, the less you can influence that teen.

Control eventually leads to resistance, and resistance to rebellion. Then we get nowhere. But if we look carefully at methods of influence that enable us to lead our teens towards high self-esteem, courage and positive behavior, then we can play a powerful role in their development.

Cycle Busters

Our goal as parents is to help discouraged teens break out of their failure cycles, and to help encouraged teens continue to thrive in their success cycles. To do this requires a skillful blend of encouragement (which we'll cover in this session) and discipline (which we'll cover in the next).

Unfortunately, we can also use our influence negatively to throw a success cycle into a failure cycle. This is usually the result of constant *dis*couragement. For example, if a teen is trying his best and makes a B on a test, but his parents admonish him for not getting an A, he may eventually become discouraged and turn to negative behavior.

Cycle busting, then, can be for either better or worse. Of course, since we all have ultimate control over our own cycles, teens with sufficient self-esteem will not allow anyone (teachers, parents or peers) to put them into failure cycles. As Eleanor Roosevelt so aptly put it:

"No one can make you feel inferior without your consent."

Session II - Instilling Courage and Self-Esteem   47

Chapter 4

Encouragement: A Powerful Influence

Since most people *are* influenced by the feedback they receive from others, we want to become skilled at using our influence with our teens to *en*courage them. We want to en-courage them in the sense of instilling courage AND we want to systematically encourage them to pursue the positive approaches to their basic goals.

Avoid Discouraging

The misbehaving teen is usually a dis-couraged teen. Somewhere along the line, he or she has lost the courage to face life's problems with positive approaches. Instead, such teens have come to believe that the only path open to them is the easier, negative approach. For example, it is certainly easier to achieve the goal of power through the negative approach of rebellion, than by the positive approach of independence through responsibility. Yet for the teen who has become dis-couraged, the negative is the only chance they see of being significant.

The misbehaving teen is usually a dis-couraged teen.

Before we look at how to en-courage our teens, we want to first become aware of some common ways that we may be discouraging them. Keep in mind the Think-Feel-Do cycle, and remember that as we become discouraging events in our teens' lives, we tend to lower their self-esteem, which leads to dis-couragement, which leads to negative behavior...which may prompt us to become even more punishing and discouraging. To bust this cycle, see which, if any, of these common discouraging influences you need to learn to avoid:

- **Negative Expectations.** If somebody who is important to you doesn't believe in your ability, you probably won't believe in it either. They don't have to say so; you can usually tell what they think of you by the way they act around you and the words they use with you. You pick up on those things pretty easily. Of course, sometimes they make their opinions of you pretty clear by saying such things as:

"I can't see wasting money on guitar lessons when you probably won't stick with it anyway."

"If I let you spend the night with Cary, you two will just get into trouble."

- **Focusing on Mistakes.** If somebody who is important to you spends a lot of time telling you what you do wrong, you come to believe that there is more wrong with you than right. It becomes harder to do things right because you are paying so much attention to your mistakes and blunders.

"I notice that you forgot your glass in the den again last night. Would you please be more considerate?"

"Gosh, honey, I thought you knew your lines. This is the second time I've had to prompt you."

■ **Perfectionism.** If your parents expect more from you than you are able to give, then you gradually stop trying, because you know you will never be able to satisfy them. You may decide to make your mark in other ways, like misbehaving. Since you can't be the best at being the best, maybe you will set your goal at being the best at being the worst.

Or maybe you decide to take perfection to a harmful extreme. For example, maybe you decide to become perfect at losing weight, so you become anorexic. In fact, many types of eating disorders are considered a product of perfectionism.

"There's just no excuse for a girl as pretty as you being even a pound over-weight."

"Just keep in mind that nobody comes to see the person who finishes second."

■ **Overprotection.** If somebody who to you is important spends too much time telling you how dangerous and difficult the world is, you come to believe that you can't handle things for yourself, so you let them handle things for you. If you get in trouble at school or with the law, they are there to bail you out. And since you never experience the consequences of your mistakes, you begin to get the idea that you can do anything you like. But you strangely find yourself not feeling very confident, though you may act over-confident to make up for it.

"Sure, I'll be glad to go down to the school and talk to your teacher. I'm sure when she realizes how hard you worked, she'll change your grade."

"Listen, I know what boys are up to, and there's just no way that you're going to start dating until you're a senior."

Turning Discouragement into Encouragement

You have just read four main ways that parents (and teachers) often discourage teens. Fortunately, these dis-couragers can be turned around to become ways of en-couraging our teens:

HOW TO DISCOURAGE	HOW TO ENCOURAGE
1. Have negative expectations.	1. Show confidence.
2. Focus on mistakes.	2. Build on strengths.
3. Expect perfection.	3. Value the teen.
4. Give too much protection.	4. Stimulate independence.

Let's look more closely at these ways of encouraging, which, by the way, work just as well in work situations and adult-adult relationships:

1. How to Show Confidence:

A cornerstone of self-esteem and courage is the belief that we are capable. As we achieve successes in solving life's problems and mastering new skills, our belief in ourselves grows. But tackling problems and attempting new skills takes confidence. Parents can help by showing this confidence in their teens. Here are some ways to do this:

Giving your teen responsibility is a nonverbal way of showing confidence.

■ **Give responsibility.** Giving your teen responsibility is a nonverbal way of showing confidence. It is a way of saying, "I know that you can do this." Of course, you want to give responsibilities in line with what you know about your teen's abilities, or the standards may be set too high. Here are some examples of giving responsibility in ways that demonstrate confidence:

"Since you have handled getting yourself up in the morning so well, we think you can handle the responsibility of setting your own bedtime."

"We will agree to your going to the party if you will agree that if there is any alcohol or drugs being used, you will call us to pick you up immediately."

■ **Ask your teen's opinion or advice.** Older children and teens like to have parents lean on their knowledge or judgment. When you ask your teen's opinion, you are demonstrating confidence in his ability to make a useful contribution. If you ask your teen to teach you something, it shows confidence in his knowledge and skills. Asking for his opinions in such ways helps bolster his feelings of self-esteem:

"I've been thinking about buying a computer for the home. Would you help us all learn how to use it?"

"Now that you'll be dating soon, we'd like your help in setting some guidelines so that we can all feel comfortable with the situation."

■ **Avoid the temptation to rescue.** It is an act of confidence in our teen's abilities when we refuse to step in and take over when she becomes discouraged. What a temptation it is, this tendency to relieve her discomfort by doing the thing that is so hard for her and so easy for us! But when we give in to the temptation, we are not showing confidence in the teen. If we do something for the teen on a regular basis that she, with a little persistence, could do independently, then we are communicating that we do not have confidence in her ability to follow a task through to the end. When we bail her out of the consequences of misbehavior, we rob her of an important lesson in responsibility. We say in effect that we don't have confidence in her ability to handle the consequences of her actions.

All in all, rescuing is not a way to encourage teenagers who are discouraged, it is a way to certify their discouragement. Such teens often show an inability to tolerate frustration. When things don't work out immediately, they give up — often having a "frustration tantrum."

"Keep trying, you can do it!"

"No, I can't stop the kids from picking on you. But I can talk to you about some things that you can do."

2. How to Build on the Teen's Strengths:

I learned an important lesson as a young counselor of adolescents: "If you want a teenager to get better, find something about that teenager that you like." Focusing our attention on what's right with our teens, rather than what is wrong, is tremendously encouraging. And, as we've seen, encouragement leads to improved self-esteem which leads to courage and positive behavior...in other words, a success cycle.

We can also build on strengths to teach specific skills and character traits. Whether it is helping a teen learn to complete his homework, or teaching him to be honest, we can systematically build on strengths to accomplish this. Three steps are important:

■ **Acknowledge what they do well.** Once you know where you would like the teen to end up (for example, having good study habits or being an honest individual), get an idea where the teen is on the A to Z journey towards reaching that goal. It is unlikely that he can't read a word or that he answers every question with a lie; he will be somewhere between A and Z. Now you have a place to start. Acknowledge what he *can do*.

"This is terrific! You've completed every assignment. This is the way to get ahead at school. I can really see that you've worked hard at this, but then I know you can work hard...I've seen you on the basketball court."

"I'm not thrilled that you borrowed my saw without asking, but I do appreciate your owning up to it when I asked. I appreciate the honesty."

"Catch 'em being good."

It is much more effective to "catch 'em being good" than our traditional approach of catching them being bad. In addition to focusing on the systematic A to Z course, it also helps to acknowledge other areas where the teen is already experiencing some success. This helps build the self-esteem that translates into risk taking and other successes. The parent who brought in the basketball connection in the previous example was using this strength building technique effectively.

Examples like the following offer teens a healthy diet of encouragement:

"It was a real pleasure having you out to dinner tonight. And I don't just mean your manners, though you were a perfect gentleman. I was thinking more of your sense of humor; you really have developed quite a wit."

"Thank you for helping with the yard. It looks great!"

"I appreciate your playing the stereo quietly while I took a nap. That was very considerate."

"Thanks for getting in on time. I appreciate it."

- **Encourage taking the next step.** Teens get a sense of self-esteem from attaining excellence at something, whether it be a sport, a school subject, or a skill. To achieve excellence, however, requires many steps (A to Z) and much improvement. It also requires risk, because with each new step, there is the potential for failure. Even with teens who have strong self-esteem, there are times when their fear of failure paralyzes them, making it difficult for them to take the next step. And there are times for all of us when the frustration of not progressing the way we'd like undermines our courage and tempts us to give up. This is when an encouraging word from a parent, teacher or coach can help give the teen enough courage to take the risk. For example:

"Learning to do algebra can be frustrating, and I know you feel like giving up. But if you'll just stick with it, I know you'll get it. Look how far you've come already! Now, what do you say you tackle that last problem again?"

"I know it hasn't been easy, but you've really improved in being honest with us. And we're feeling like we can trust you more. Now, if we let you go to that party Saturday night, will you agree to call us to come get you if there is any alcohol or drugs being used?"

- **Concentrate on improvement, not perfection.** The mistake most people make in the encouragement process is to wait until the teen attains the desired result (Z on the A to Z line) before offering praise or encouragement. The key to encouragement, however, is to break the process down into a lot of small steps, offering encouragement along the entire route. Any improvement, no matter how small, is a step in the right direction, and should be noticed. Since success is a great motivator, we want the teen to be able to experience numerous successes along the way. This builds self-esteem and keeps the teen moving towards the goal. If the teen falls back a step, and that's usual along the way, she needs our encouragement to keep at it and not give up. In fact, her effort alone, even when she's not making progress, can still be encouraged.

"Great! You are really getting good at writing down all of your assignments. One more day and you'll have a whole week."

"Thanks for telling us about cutting practice last week. That took a lot of courage. We'll talk about what to do about it in a minute, but first I want you to know how much we admire your efforts to be more honest."

"I can really see the effort that went into this."

"Hey, this room is really looking good! You've gotten all your magazines picked up, and the bed's even made. If you like, I have some time and could help you figure out a system for organizing your closet."

3. How to Value the Teen:

A teen's self-esteem does not spring from achievements alone. Much more important for most people is that they are accepted by significant people in their lives. In fact, much success hunting is really aimed at trying to win the acceptance of those significant people. Ironically, what most of us really want down deep inside is to be accepted for ourselves, *not* just for our achievements.

Teens who feel accepted by their parents have a tremendous bedrock of self-esteem.

Teens who feel accepted by their parents have a tremendous bedrock of self-esteem upon which to construct a healthy, happy life. Without it, some of the richest, most successful people in history have lived lives of quiet desperation, wondering why their successes were never satisfying.

The goal is to communicate to our teens that win or lose, pass or fail, in trouble or out of trouble, we are still their parents AND WE ARE GLAD OF IT. We all need this unconditional regard from someone, and if we don't get it from our parents, then we need to get it someplace else: from a substitute parent, a therapist or religion.

This is why parenting programs that advocate kicking a rebellious teen out of the house are off the mark. We never want to communicate that the teen is no longer part of the family. We want to communicate just the opposite: "No matter what it takes, counseling, hospitalization or the outdoor program, we're going to find a way for you to be a contributing member of this family. We love you, and we're going to help you get the help you need."

Fortunately, for most families it doesn't come to this. But we all need to look at the subtle messages that we give our teens, and focus on ways of valuing them just because they are *our* teens. Here are some ways of doing just that:

■ **Separate worth from accomplishments.** A teen's worth is less a matter of what he or she *does,* and more a matter of who he or she *is.* You can let your teens know that while you admire their successes and share their disappointment in their failures, you love them for themselves. You can put emphasis on the activities themselves, and not just on the results. You can encourage your teen while he is doing a task instead of waiting until the task is completed.

"I'm glad you enjoy learning."

"It's nice to get good grades, especially when you've put so much effort into it."

"Playing your hardest is more important than winning."

"Losing doesn't make a person a loser."

■ **Separate worth from misbehavior.** Just as a teen's worth is something different from the sum total of her accomplishments, so is it different from her mistakes or failures. There are no bad teens, only bad behavior. If a teen is labeled "bad," or "no good," she may eventually come to believe that the label is true. When this happens, bad behavior then becomes appropriate; after all, what should we expect from "bad" people but "bad" behavior? For this reason, it is important that we refrain from labeling teens, and actually correct the teen when we hear her referring to herself as "bad" or "no good."

Mistakes, like misbehavior, are not indications of a lack of worth, but are actually part of growth and development. A mistake can teach a valuable lesson, showing a teen what not to do in the future. We want to help teens, especially perfectionistic teens, learn to make friends with their mistakes. Mistakes, as we have said, are tools for learning.

Teens, and adults, who are afraid of

being imperfect actually retard their own growth and development. A perfectionist, according to one definition, is a person who won't attempt a foreign language until he can speak it fluently. As this quip implies, a fear of mistakes yields a fear of trying, which in turn yields less learning. Since one of our goals is to help teens learn, we want to help them accept mistakes with a smile rather than a kick.

"So you made a mistake. Let's see what you can learn from it."

"I don't agree that you're a 'screw-up' as you put it. I do agree that you messed up, but I see it as a mistake in judgment. I know you. You'll take it to heart and learn from the experience."

"We love you a lot, so things have got to change. We just can't stand by and watch someone we care so much about destroy herself with drugs."

■ **Appreciate the teen's uniqueness.** Although it is important to teach teens that all people are equal, that doesn't mean that all people are the same. It is encouraging for your teen to know that he is unique, special, one of a kind. You can appreciate your teen's uniqueness by taking an interest in his activities. Most of all, you can say and do things that show your teen that you love him for his unique self, and for no other reason.

"Anyway, that's my opinion, what's yours?"

"When I see you from a distance, I can tell it's you from your walk."

"This room is really you! I could never have decorated it for you."

"You are the only you in the whole world. What luck that you happen to be my daughter!"

"I love you."

4. How to Stimulate Independence:

The last thing we want to do as parents is to keep our teens overly dependent on us.

Independence, or the ability to stand on one's own two feet, is essential for thriving in our democratic society. In fact, when we keep our teens overly dependent on us, we pay a price; as psychologist Haim Ginott once wrote, "Dependence breeds hostility." The last thing we want to do as parents is to keep our teens overly dependent on us. (Unless, of course, you want to someday have a hostile 30-year-old playing rock-and-roll and living in your guest room.)

As we encourage our teens towards independence, we also want to keep in mind that they will benefit enormously by learning to cooperate. "No man is an island" expresses the truth that interdependence — independent individuals choosing to work together cooperatively — offers the best chance for success for both the individual and the human community.

Parents can encourage teens to become both independent and interdependent. We can stimulate them to rely on their own abilities and efforts, and to contribute those abilities cooperatively to working, playing and associating with others.

■ **Avoid pampering your teen.** When parents put themselves into the teen's service or otherwise treat the teen like a privileged character, the teen eventually becomes dependent, spoiled and discouraged. Some signs of pampering include: Calling her more than once to get up in the morning; routinely driving the teen places on short notice; picking out her clothes; giving her money on demand instead of an allowance; allowing the teen to curse you or otherwise speak disrespectfully; making your teen's homework your responsibility; allowing her to eat meals in front of the TV; cleaning up after her; not requiring her to help with family chores; and rescuing her from the consequences of her misbehavior.

If you find some of these examples hitting home, then you can let your teen know that you have decided to stop pampering her, and begin treating her more respectfully. You can do this in a firm yet friendly way, taking responsibility yourself, while even encouraging the teen. For example:

"I want to apologize to you for treating you like you didn't have the good sense to handle _____(e.g., getting yourself up in the morning; your own money; your own homework; picking up your own clothes). From now on, I'm going to stop treating you like a baby, and leave that up to you."

"I don't use that kind of language when I'm angry with you; I don't expect you to use it when you are angry with me."

"I'll be glad to show you where dirty clothes go, but from now on I'm only washing the clothes that get put there."

"We'd be glad to discuss getting you a private phone line. Of course, we would expect you to help pay for it."

■ **Help the teen develop a sense of interdependence.** Because belonging is a basic goal of all humans, it deserves special emphasis. You can invite co-operative behavior on the part of your teen, with the aim of letting him experience the pleasure and benefits of group efforts.

"You're an important part of this family, and we'd like your input at family council meetings."

"Would you like to help me put together the new gas grill?"

"Would you like to make lasagna with us?"

Family Enrichment Activity #2

"Letter of Encouragement"

As a young Sunday School teacher, I became annoyed with the idea of having to give grades to my students. Grades seemed an inadequate way to express either their progress or the way that I felt about them after having shared nine months with them. I decided to write each of my students a personal letter to go with the grades. While writing the letters, I found myself describing the positive aspects of each child and how he or she was progressing. These "letters of encouragement" were received appreciatively as the children left for summer vacation.

I didn't think much more about the letters until four years later. I was at a reception when a woman approached me and introduced herself as the mother of one of my students from that same Sunday School class. "That letter you wrote Alice," she said, "meant so much to her. You know she still has it on her bulletin board."

All of the encouragement skills discussed in this session could be considered as family enrichment activities. But somehow "putting it in writing" carries extra weight in our society. In addition, the child can refer back to a letter of encouragement in the future and rekindle the warm feeling that it generated, just as Alice did.

This week's activity is to write a letter of encouragement to each of your children. Let your letter have the following characteristics:

■ Write about his or her improvement in some area, not necessarily perfection.

■ Write only truthful statements; don't say that the child has improved when he or she really hasn't.

■ Be specific about what the improvements are.

■ Say how the teen's behavior has been helpful to others.

Example: A parent's letter to a child might look like this:

Dear Sean,

It's a thrill to see my first-born child growing into the healthy, capable young man you are becoming. I am enjoying watching you develop talents and abilities that are uniquely yours, and seeing the satisfaction you are getting from drawing and from track. I can just picture your Mars Bars cartoon strip running in the Sunday paper someday.

I really appreciate the effort you are making to keep up with your chores, with fewer and fewer reminders. It's a help to know we can count on you, and your contributions to the family mean a lot. The yard really looks great since you've taken it over!

Thanks for being you.

Love,
Mom

"Letter of Encouragement"

Session

II

Remember When...

Recall a time when one of your parents said or did something that you found encouraging when you were a teen. Take a moment to visualize the experience and to rekindle the positive feeling it provided.

What did your parent do or say?

_____

How did you feel?

_____

Now, try to recall a letter or note that you found encouraging...from your parents or someone else.

What encouraged you about it?

_____

Use this space to write a rough draft of a letter of encouragement to each of your teens. Then copy the letter on stationery or other good paper before placing it where your teen will find it, or mailing it to him or her.

_____

_____

_____

_____

_____

_____

_____

_____

Discouragement to Encouragement

Discouraging Influences*	Put yourself in the child's place; what would you probably...		
	THINK	FEEL	DO
SCENE 1 (Choosing friends)			
SCENE 2 (The report card)			
Encouraging Influences			
SCENE 3 (Choosing friends)			
SCENE 4 (The report card)			

*Discouraging Influences

■ Focusing on mistakes
■ Perfectionism
■ Negative expectations
■ Overprotection

Encouraging Influences

■ Building on strengths
■ Showing confidence
■ Valuing the teen
■ Stimulating independence

Encouragement Profile

We all have abilities, talents and qualities which are useful and which are learned. Think about these qualities in your own family and write some of them below, filling in the name of your teen or teens as you go.

_____ does well at _____ .

I do well at _____ .

_____ helps me _____ .

Something _____ is learning: _____ .

Something I am learning: _____ .

A strength _____ has is _____ .

One of my strengths is _____ .

_____ can _____ .

I can _____ .

_____ learned how to _____ .

What I like best about _____ is _____ .

What I like best about me is _____ .

NOTE: The more you look for your teen's positive traits, the easier it becomes.

Encouragement Chart

Practice using encouraging statements this week. To help you stay aware of your own efforts to be more encouraging, use the chart below to give yourself a check each time you make an encouraging statement.

TEEN'S NAME	DAY	ENCOURAGING STATEMENTS
_____	_____	_____
_____	_____	_____
_____	_____	_____
_____	_____	_____
_____	_____	_____
_____	_____	_____
_____	_____	_____
_____	_____	_____
_____	_____	_____
_____	_____	_____
_____	_____	_____
_____	_____	_____
_____	_____	_____
_____	_____	_____
_____	_____	_____

Stimulating Independence

Think of things that you are now doing for your teens that they could be doing for themselves. For example, making their bed, picking up their clothes, cleaning up after them, etc. Make a list below:

1. _____

2. _____

3. _____

4. _____

Now, choose one of these to let your teen do for himself or herself this week. Be sure to be encouraging as you turn this over to your teen, and practice your encouragement skills as your teen progresses.

Afterwards...

What did you like about how it went?

_____

_____

_____

What can you do to improve things next time?

_____

_____

_____

Developing
Responsibility

Chapter 5

Handling
Problems

There was a young man who was desperate for work. He had never had a job before, and though he was 27 years old, his parents were still supporting him. They had finally had enough of his dependency, as well as their own overprotection, and had given him three months to find a job. When he saw after 10 weeks that they were serious about pushing him out of the nest, he began seriously beating the pavement for work.

He failed. He had never been taught to do things for himself, and had not developed the skills to find a job. His father, as usual, came to his rescue and called a friend in the construction business who arranged for his son to have a good-paying job driving a dump truck. On the first day of his first job, the young man backed the dump truck over an embankment. When confronted by the foreman, and asked how he could do such a reckless thing, the young man replied, "Well, nobody told me not to."

This chapter and the next will present methods of handling problems and misbehavior when they occur in a family. But this chapter is also about something much more basic to the development of a teen's ability to thrive in our democratic society. It is about RESPONSIBILITY.

Responsibility

How much responsibility for the course of our lives do we accept? If the answer is "less than total responsibility," then we are cheating ourselves. The more responsible we become, the more effective and satisfied with our circumstances we also become.

Why do we avoid responsibility if this is so? Because we are afraid of being blamed or punished for making mistakes. Who would blame or punish us? Sometimes it is critical people with whom we live or work. But even their criticism would be harmless if it were not for the fact that we blame and punish ourselves the hardest.

Where did we learn this self-criticism? Most of us learned it a long time ago from our parents, many of whom believed in the autocratic or permissive methods of parenting, and the blame and criticism that went with these styles.

How do we avoid responsibility? We blame others for our mistakes and failures, or we blame circumstances, because it is too painful to accept responsibility ourselves and suffer the self-criticism we insist on dishing out. We say, "You made

Responsibility is the process of making choices and then accepting the consequences of those choices.

me late," or, "You made me angry." Or we justify our failings: "Being late isn't such a big deal;" "I have a bad temper; " "I'm a Leo; " "I'm an alcoholic;" "I'm just no good;" "Nobody told me not to."

How can we help prepare teens for responsible adulthood? The first step is for us to resist the temptation to blame and punish them for their mistakes and misbehavior. These techniques actually influence them to avoid responsibility — to blame and justify. This chapter is about other methods of disciplining teens, methods that teach responsibility while they help you handle everyday problems. But first, let's look at what responsibility really is: *Responsibility is the process of making choices and then accepting the consequences of those choices.*

The most effective and the most satisfied people have learned how to make choices and how to accept responsibility for whatever happens as a result of their choices. If the consequence is a good one, then they have a good model for making a similar choice in the future. If the consequence is a bad one, then they know better how to choose next time and avoid the same bad consequences. Either way, they learn and grow. And this is the way teens learn and grow, too.

In this chapter, we will look at some effective, tried-and-true methods which parents have used to help their teens grow in their ability to make responsible choices. But first, let's look at the circumstances in which choices are made.

Freedom and the Limits to Freedom

A choice can be made only when there is freedom to choose; otherwise, the choice is no choice at all. For if the person is not free to choose, we have to assume that someone else has already made the choice for the person. An essential condition for responsibility, therefore, is the freedom to choose.

Autocratic parents give their teens almost no freedom to make choices. They believe that since teens are inexperienced at knowing what the limits are, it is the parents who must make the choices for them, thus helping them avoid the pain and the pitfalls of poor choices. Parents who follow an autocratic model of parenting stifle the teen's ability to handle responsibility. He eventually rebels against their harsh suppression of his growth, and he remains inexperienced at making choices on his own.

Permissive parents, perhaps in reaction to their own autocratic upbringing, follow a model of parenting that resembles anarchy, allowing their teens unlimited freedom and permission to choose to do whatever they want. Yet, teens do not learn responsibility any better in these circumstances than in an autocratic home.

A young man executed in the electric chair for the murder of a woman and her three small children reported that he would probably do it again if he had the chance, because he came from a home where no one ever told him not to do certain things. He had grown up without limits — free to do whatever he pleased. And was he happy about this? Hardly. He chose the electric chair instead of imprisonment because he described his life as a "living hell!"

So teens clamor for freedom to make their own choices, while parents call for limits to that freedom, and the dialogue becomes a universal chant, repeated the world over:

> "Freedom!"

> "Limits."

> "FREEDOM!"

> "LIMITS!"

Active parents are acutely aware of their teens' need for freedom, but freedom within well-defined limits.

Fortunately, there is a third alternative — what we are calling the "active" approach. Active parents are acutely aware of their teens' need for freedom, but freedom within well-defined limits. They work hard to set limits that are in line with the teen's age and level of responsibility, aware that over-restrictive limits lead to sneaking around and other forms of rebellion, and that limits that are too loose lead to selfish and destructive behavior.

This concept of "freedom within expanding limits" suggests that a 2-year-old will make fewer of her own decisions than a 9-year-old, who again will make fewer decisions than a 17-year-old. In fact, the ideal situation for a teen spending her last year at home is for the teen to make almost all of her own decisions. The parent has become almost like a roommate and consultant. This makes sense when we consider that our goal is to prepare teenagers for independent living, and soon we won't be around to offer any limits.

Like most things, teaching responsibility is a gradual A-to-Z process. This chapter will present proven techniques for accomplishing this. It involves giving children choices, and then allowing them to experience the consequences of those choices. It also means involving them in family decision making and problem solving.

The Problem-Handling Model
for Parents

The difference between successful families and those constantly in pain and turmoil is *not* the presence or absence of problems. All families have problems and conflicts, and all teenagers present challenges. The difference is in the ability of the family to successfully handle their problems so that learning occurs. The following diagram depicts a successful method of dealing with family problems.

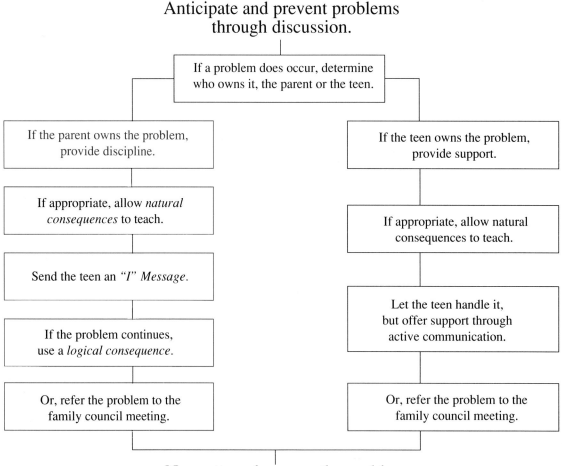

Anticipate and prevent problems through discussion.

If a problem does occur, determine who owns it, the parent or the teen.

If the parent owns the problem, provide discipline.	If the teen owns the problem, provide support.
If appropriate, allow *natural consequences* to teach.	If appropriate, allow natural consequences to teach.
Send the teen an *"I" Message*.	Let the teen handle it, but offer support through active communication.
If the problem continues, use a *logical consequence*.	
Or, refer the problem to the family council meeting.	Or, refer the problem to the family council meeting.

No matter who owns the problem, offer encouragement.

As you may have noticed, these same skills that we use to handle everyday family problems are also the skills that enable us to teach our teens courage, responsibility and cooperation. In this session, we will cover problem prevention, problem ownership, natural and logical consequences, and "I" Messages. Then in Session IV, we'll deal with active communication and the family council meeting.

Who Owns the Problem?

This may seem a strange question to ask. Autocratic parents tend to act as if they own all of the problems in the family, and that they are responsible for deciding what will be done to solve them. Permissive parents tend to take on too little responsibility for problems, and allow their teens too much choice.

The active parent, however, understands that there are some problems that belong to the teen, and that the teen should be free to decide how he or she will handle them. In those cases the active parent may offer support and encouragement, but will not take over the problem. The active parent also understands the need for discipline when the problem belongs to the parent.

We can usually determine who owns a problem by asking three questions:

- With whom is this behavior or situation interfering directly?
- Who is raising the issue or making the complaint?
- Whose purposes are being thwarted by the problem?

Let's look at some examples to help clarify this concept:

Situation	Who owns the problem?	Why?
Teen drives the car into the garage too fast.	Parent	It's the parent's responsibility to teach teens to drive safely.
Teen complains about her younger sister going into her room without permission.	Teen	Siblings have the right to have relationships with each other without parental intervention. They need to learn to relate to each other on their own.
Teen forgets to do his family chore.	Parent	This affects everyone in the family, including the parents.
Teen comes in late for curfew.	Parent	Parents have a responsibility to supervise their teens. This goal has been thwarted.
Teen complains that her teacher gave her an unfair grade.	Teen	Schoolwork is the teen's responsibility. Her goal has been thwarted.

Problem Prevention Through Discussion

Many shrewd teens operate under the belief that it is often easier to obtain forgiveness than permission. We can discourage this "act now, ask questions later" mentality by initiating problem solving discussions with our teens *before* a problem occurs. For example, your teen has just received her driver's license, and wants to borrow your car. Many related conflicts and problems can be avoided by sitting down together (preferably with both parents in a two-parent family) and setting up guidelines.

The process is one of discussion and negotiation.

The process *is not* one of laying down the law or otherwise informing the teen of *your* guidelines. The process is one of discussion and negotiation in which together you arrive at a set of guidelines that you both agree upon. As in any negotiation, you will have points that are essential to you, and are *not negotiable*. This is part of your parental responsibility in setting limits. But within those limits you can win cooperation by being flexible and together you can arrive at decisions that everyone thinks are fair. The result of this discussion will be clear limits; the teen will know what is expected of her and she will be clear as to the consequences for violating those limits.

Problem Prevention/Problem Solving Discussion Method

Step 1. Define the problem or potential problems.

Think about all of the questions that relate to the topic, and anticipate where problems might occur. These are the areas where you and your teen will need to agree on guidelines. For example, with the car, some of the questions will be:

- When will the teen have use of the car?
- Who pays for gas, insurance, and repairs?
- What does the teen need to know about the insurance policy number, the agent, and what to do if there is an accident?
- Does the teen know how to change a flat tire?
- Does the teen know not to hitchhike for help after a breakdown? (Many teens are abducted and killed hitching each year.)
- What about wearing seat belts?
- Who may drive the car or ride in it?
- Is your teen aware of the dangers of driving after drinking and your attitude on the subject? (More on this critical topic in Session V.)

- WHAT ARE THE CONSEQUENCES IF THE TEEN DOES NOT FOLLOW THE GUIDELINES?

Step 2. Share thoughts and feelings about the problem.

Once you and your teen have clarified the problems and potential problems, share your thoughts and feelings about the issue. This gives each of you a chance to express what is important to you and to become aware of what is important to the other. Remember, freedom of expression is a hallmark of Active Parenting, just as it is the foundation of life in a democratic society.

For example, Mother says, "My number one concern is for your safety, and anything that we agree on has to be safe."

Step 3. Generate possible solutions through brainstorming.

The key to brainstorming is to generate as many possible solutions as possible *without* evaluation. When people are working together cooperatively, one idea will generate another so that the group comes up with possibilities that none of the individuals alone could have produced.

Step 4. Arrive at a decision through discussion.

The goal of the discussion is to reach a decision by consensus.

The goal of the discussion is to reach a decision by consensus. Consensus means that the solution may not be anyone's first choice, but it is a choice everyone can live with. For example, dad may want the teen to buy all of his own gas; mom may have grown up in a family where gas was provided and not think the teen should pay for any; the teen may not know what to think. A consensus might be for the teen to get a small gas allowance each week. Another decision might be for the teen to buy his own gas, but for the parents to pay for auto insurance (with the stipulation that if the teen has an accident or moving violation that causes the rates to go up, he has to pay for the rate hike). The possibilities are endless, and when the focus is on finding solutions that satisfy everyone (rather than on winning arguments), this kind of decision making is a creative and effective form of negotiation.

You will have some non-negotiable areas.

Again, you will have some non-negotiable areas. For example, no drinking and driving. These non-negotiable points should be health or safety matters of significant importance, and not just what you think is best for your teen. Sometimes you can agree to negotiate within limits. For example, you are non-negotiable about the need for a curfew, but you can still negotiate what that curfew will be, the exceptions that can be made, and other related issues. Remember, the goal is to neither dictate (autocratic) nor give in (permissive). The active parent is willing to discuss, and thereby allow the teen to influence the decisions that affect his or her life. This teaches responsibility and heightens the chances that the teen will abide by the guidelines.

Step 5. Decide on logical consequences for violating the agreed upon guidelines.

The specifics of logical consequences will be discussed later in this session. The goal is to establish beforehand what consequence will occur if the teen breaks an agreement. For example, a first violation might result in loss of the car for a week. More serious violations, such as drinking and driving, might mean that the teen cannot use the car for a longer period.

Step 6. Put the decision into action.

Some families choose to write agreements down, often in a log book, so that memory doesn't distort the guidelines. Once everyone does agree, the action can be carried out.

Step 7. Follow up.

For guidelines and rules to be of value in the long run, they must be enforced. Parents will need to be respectfully aware of their teen's behavior, so that they will know whether the agreements are being kept. For example, to follow up with the no drinking and driving guideline (in Session V we'll talk about a general "no use" of alcohol and other drugs rule), the parent must be awake when the teen comes home at night.

What about trust? Teens who consistently abide by their agreements can be trusted more, and parents do not need to follow up as often. Teens who often break their agreements need regular follow up until they establish a new track record. Be straight with your teen about this, and don't be intimidated by the old, "Don't you trust me?" routine. (The answer to this is, "I trust you as far as your behavior indicates I should.") If your teen has not kept agreements well, you can add, "Right now, because you broke curfew by 45 minutes last Saturday without calling, I think I need to follow up a little more closely for a while." If the teen has behaved responsibly within the guidelines, you can offer encouragement by saying something like, "You've done a good job of sticking to our agreements, and you've earned our trust. Here's a door key so that you can let yourself in at night when we've already gone to bed."

Chapter 6

Effective
Discipline

You may recall that in Session I we presented the case against the use of punishment as a means of influencing teens in our modern society. We suggested that punishment (the idea that you have to hurt the teen to teach him) often leads to resentment and revenge. Although problems may seem to get better in the short run, they usually become worse later on. In addition, punishment teaches nothing about responsibility, only about doing what you are told, or, more often, finding sneaky ways not to get caught.

In this session we will look at discipline methods that are more effective, as well as more respectful. These methods will give you tools for influencing your teens towards positive behavior, and at the same time will help them develop the important quality of responsibility.

There are three key things to keep in mind throughout this chapter:

1. Our goal is to teach our teens, not to hurt them. In fact, the word "discipline" itself comes from the Latin word "disciplina" meaning "instruction." Of course, our teens may not like our instructions or the consequences that we may apply; however, they will not suffer hurt to either their bodies or their self-esteem in the process.

2. Whenever we discipline a negative behavior, we should always want to find opportunities to encourage the positive alternative and to show acceptance of the teen as a person.

3. When using discipline to influence our teens, we always use the least assertive method that will work. That means not using a hand grenade to kill a mosquito.

Polite Requests

Not every problem or conflict requires a full-fledged discussion or firm discipline. Often, a polite request is enough to influence a teen to change behavior (especially if the relationship is already a positive one).

When a teen doesn't know what we want in a situation, the first step is to politely make our desires known through a request. For example, you have decided that you no longer want to pamper your teen by picking up his dirty dishes left over from his snacking in the den. Your polite request might be, "Honey, from now on will you do me a favor and bring your dishes to the sink when you're through with your snack?" If your teen agrees, be sure to add, "Thanks, that will be a big help." Now, this may seem so simple that it sounds condescending, but I promise you that we parents do talk to teens in ways that would be clearly disrespectful if used with other adults. The parent in the above example could easily wait until she is fed up with being a slave, hold it inside for another week to let it really boil, then burst out with, "I'm sick and tired of having to pick up your mess! What do you think I am, your slave? If you weren't so lazy and inconsiderate...." None of which is likely to produce responsibility, cooperation or dishes in the sink.

If a teen does comply with our polite request, but slips up, we can offer a friendly reminder, "Honey, I notice you forgot to put your dishes in the sink. Please come get them."

When a teen repeatedly forgets to keep an agreement, when she isn't putting out the effort or is taking a negative approach to one of the five goals, then a stronger communication is called for.

"I" Messages

"I" Messages, a term coined by psychologist Tom Gordon in his pioneering Parent Effectiveness Training (P.E.T.) program, are firm and friendly communications that can produce surprisingly effective results. They are called "I" Messages because they shift the emphasis from the teen (a traditional "you" message) to how the parent ("I") feels about the teen's behavior. They do these things:

- They allow the parent to say how he or she feels about the teen's behavior without blaming or labeling the teen.

- They create a situation in which the teen is more likely to hear what the parent is saying because it is expressed in a nonthreatening way.

- They convey clearly to the teen one consequence (the parent's feeling) of the teen's behavior.

- They put the emphasis on the parent's feeling about the teen's *behavior*, and *not* on the teen's *personality*.

- They give the teen clear information about what change in behavior the parent wants.

When to use an "I" Message:

"I" Messages are only effective when the parent owns the problem. When a polite request has failed to change behavior, an "I" Message is a more assertive next step. If the problem remains after an "I" Message, then the use of logical consequences provides a third level of assertiveness.

"I" Messages work best in a firm and calm tone of voice.

Since "I" Messages work best in a firm and *calm* tone of voice, avoid using them when you are too angry. Allow for a cooling-off period, then approach your teen when you have regained control. An angry "I" Message can easily trigger rebellion in a power seeking teen, especially when delivered aggressively, rather than assertively.

How to send an "I" Message:

There are four parts to an "I" Message:

1. Name the behavior or situation you want changed.

As we said in Session II on encouragement, it is important to separate the deed from the doer. It isn't that the teen is bad, only that we have a problem with something the teen is doing. By beginning with a statement aimed at the behavior, we avoid attacking the teen's personality and self-esteem, thereby reducing the risk of defensiveness. We begin this part with, "When you..."

For example, "When you leave dirty dishes in the den..."

2. Say how you feel about the situation.

This lets the teen know that the problem is serious to you (without your resorting to yelling and screaming). Although parents often use the word "angry" to de-

scribe their feelings, this is often a mask for two other emotions: "fear" and "hurt." Teens can usually hear us better when we are expressing these emotions, because they are less threatening. "I feel concerned" or "I feel hurt" may be closer to the truth, as well as more effective.

This part of the "I" Message begins with "I feel..."

For example, "I feel taken advantage of..."

3. State your reason.

Nobody likes to be treated as if he or she were expected to be *blindly* obedient. If we are going to change what is comfortable to us to please an authority, we at least want that authority to have a good reason. Teenagers are no exception. A simple explanation about how the teen's behavior is interfering with your purposes is called for. It can begin, "because..."

For example, "because I have to spend time and energy cleaning up behind you."

4. Say what you want done.

You have already made a polite request or two, so now you are getting more assertive. This means letting your teen know exactly what you would like done. Remember, you get more of what you ask for than what you don't ask for. This step can begin with "I want" or "I would like."

For example, "I would like you to bring your dirty dishes to the kitchen and put them in the dishwasher when you leave the den."

Putting this "I" Message all together, we have:

"When you leave dirty dishes in the den I feel taken advantage of because I have to spend time and energy cleaning up behind you. I would like you to bring your dirty dishes to the kitchen and put them in the dishwasher when you leave the den."

"I" Messages: Two Variations

1. Getting agreement: "Will you please..."

We can make an "I" Message even stronger by getting an agreement from the teen about the behavior that we want changed. This can be done following the "I" Message by simply adding the question, "Will you do that?" and then not moving until you get a "yes." This can also be done by changing the last step of the "I" Message from "I would like..." to "Will you please...?"

For example:

"When you leave dirty dishes in the den I feel taken advantage of because I have to spend time and energy cleaning up behind you. *Will you please bring your dirty dishes to the kitchen and put them in the dishwasher when you leave the den?*"

2. Establishing a time frame: "When?"

Every parent of a teenager knows the frustration of getting an agreement from the teen about doing something, finding it still not done hours later, and confronting the teen only to hear the refrain, "I'll do it." The implication of course is "I'll do it when I get around to it," and that may not occur in this century.

The solution is to get a clear agreement as to when the behavior will be completed. In the above example, the "when" is built into the phrase, "when you leave the den." Other times, it can be added right after the teen agrees to the request by simply asking, "When?"

Natural and Logical Consequences

In order to influence a teen to change from a negative behavior to a positive one, the teen first needs clear information from the parent about what change is expected. "I" Messages are a good clear way to do this. However, sometimes teens need to experience a more concrete consequence of their actions in order to learn the lesson.

What is the value of consequences?

Teens learn responsibility when they are given three things:

■ **Participation:** The opportunity to participate in setting the guidelines for their behavior.

■ **Choice:** The opportunity to choose how to behave.

■ **Consequences:** The opportunity to experience the logical results of their choice of behavior.

Consequences are powerful teachers about the effectiveness of our choices and behavior. Better than an arbitrary punishment or lecture, consequences offer parents their prime discipline tools. There are two types of consequences that will be presented: *natural consequences* and *logical consequences*.

Natural Consequences

Natural consequences are the experiences that follow naturally (that is, without parental intervention) from what teens choose to do or not do.

For example:

- The natural consequence of not putting gas into the car is running out of gas.

- The natural consequence of oversleeping on a school day is being late for school.

- The natural consequence of leaving your bicycle outside may be that it gets rusty or that it is stolen.

Natural consequences are particularly effective teachers because the parent can be a sympathetic third party, rather than the disciplinarian. Of course, to be effective we have to avoid two temptations: 1) to rescue (for example, buy him a new bike); and 2) to say "I told you so." (How much better to say, "Gee, honey, I know that's frustrating," rather than, "I told you this would happen if you didn't put that bike away!")

When Natural Consequences Cannot Be Used as Teachers

There are many situations when our best course of action is to stay out of the way and let the natural consequences teach the lesson. However, there are three circumstances in which a responsible parent cannot simply allow Mother Nature to take her toll:

1. When the natural consequences may be catastrophic. For example, the natural consequences of experimenting with drugs can be addiction or even death.

2. When the natural consequences are so far into the future that the teen is not concerned about the connection. For example, the natural consequences of not doing school work may lead to failure to graduate or fewer choices of colleges.

3. When the natural consequences of a teen's behavior affect others rather than the teen. For example, the teen returns *your* car on empty, and *you* run out of gas. In these situations the parent owns the problem, and it is up to the parent to take action to prevent such natural consequences from occurring or reoccurring.

The actions that are recommended again are:

- Problem prevention through discussion
- Polite requests
- "I" Messages
- Logical Consequences
- Family Council Meeting

Logical Consequences

Because parents cannot always rely on natural consequences, and since prevention, polite requests and "I" Messages are not always effective, logical consequences can be set up to handle parent owned problems and to teach responsibility. We call them "logical" consequences, because they are logically related to the teen's misbehavior. By definition:

Logical consequences are those results which a parent deliberately chooses to show the teen what logically follows when the teen chooses to violate family values or social requirements.

For example:

- *When Sean continues to forget to bring his dirty dishes into the kitchen after snacking in the den, he loses the privilege of taking food out of the kitchen.*

- *When Susan forgets to put gas in mom's car when she has borrowed it, she is not allowed to use the car for a week.*

Logical Consequences Versus Punishment

Logical consequences are not the same thing as punishment, even though the teen will usually experience both as unpleasant. Some of the differences are:

Logical Consequences...

...are logically connected to the misbehavior.

...are intended to teach responsible behavior.

...are administered in a firm and friendly manner.

Punishment...

...is an arbitrary retaliation for misbehavior.

...is intended to teach obedient behavior.

...is often delivered in an atmosphere of anger and resentment.

Guidelines for Using Logical Consequences

1. Give the teen a choice.

It is essential to give teens choices regarding their behavior and the consequences of their behavior. As we have emphasized, learning how to handle responsibility is learning how to make choices. Teens always choose, and the consequences of their choices teach them how to make better choices in the future. Parents can help teens in this learning process by showing them that misbehavior (that is, a negative

approach to their goals) is one of their choices, but that it brings with it logical consequences. It should also be brought out and emphasized to the teen that the other choices, the positive approach to their goals, will bring about positive consequences.

There are two types of choices that you will find extremely useful:

■ **EITHER-OR CHOICES:** These choices are usually phrased like this: "Either you may _____, or you may _____. You decide."

- **WHEN-THEN CHOICES:** These choices may be phrased like this: "When you have_____, then you may_____."

Examples of either-or choices:

- (Katherine leaves her belongings scattered around the den in the afternoon.) *"Katherine, either put your things away when you come home from school, or I'll put them in a box in the basement. You decide."* (Notice that the logical consequence of leaving her belongings lying around is the inconvenience of having to dig them out of a junk box in the basement.)

- (Calvin continues to forget to put his dirty clothes in the hamper.) *"Calvin, either put your dirty clothes in the hamper, or wash them yourself. You decide."* (The logical consequence of not putting his dirty clothes in the hamper is that he must do his own wash...or wear dirty clothes.)

Examples of when-then choices:

- (Maria has trouble getting her homework done, but likes to spend time watching TV.) *"Maria, when you have finished your homework, then you may turn on the TV."* (Notice that the logical consequence of not doing her homework is to lose the privilege of watching TV.)

- (Tom is about to leave for the swimming pool, ignoring his regular Saturday chore of mowing the lawn.) *"Tom, when you have mowed the lawn, then you may go swimming."*

Here are some poorly expressed choices. The following examples are poorly expressed because they are couched in negative terms: "Don't do that or else..." They sound like punishment.

- **POOR:** "Katherine, put your things away or I'm going to throw them in a box in the basement!"

- **POOR:** "Calvin, if you don't start putting your dirty clothes in the hamper, you're going to have to wash them yourself."

- **POOR:** "Tom, you may not go swimming until you have mowed the grass."

2. Involve the teen in a discussion to set the consequences.

Remember, life in our democratic society requires the participation of all those concerned with a problem. We stand a much better chance that the teen will cooperate with our authority if we include him or her in the decision making process. In addition, you'll be surprised how often the teen will come up with choices and solutions that we wouldn't have thought of alone.

For example: "Katherine, I still have a problem with your leaving your belongings all over the den. What do you think we can do to solve it?"

Even if the teen has no helpful suggestions or is uncooperative about finding a solution, the important thing is that you asked. Since you have invited the teen's participation, she will be less likely to think of you as a dictator, and to rebel against you. (You will want to come to the discussion prepared with your own logical consequences in case the teen has no input.)

3. Make sure the consequences are really logical.

One key to the success of logical consequences is that the consequence is *logically* connected to the misbehavior. Teens are better able to see the justice of such consequences, and will usually accept them without resentment. However, if the consequence that you select is not really related to the teen's behavior, it will come across as a punishment.

NOT LOGICAL	LOGICAL
"Either be home by 6:00 or lose your stereo for a week."	"Dinner is served at 6:00. Either be here on time or eat it cold, but by 6:30 I'm clearing the table."
"Either limit your phone calls to 15 minutes, or you're not going out Saturday."	"Either limit your phone calls to 15 minutes or give up a night using the phone each time you go over 15 minutes."
"Finish your homework or you're grounded."	"When you finish your homework every day during the week, you can go out that weekend." (This is logical if you establish a "work before play" philosophy in your family.)

4. Only give choices that you can live with.

There are many potential logical consequences for any given problem. For that reason, brainstorming with other parents, a spouse, or even the teen can help. However, when *you* own the problem, it is up to you to decide which choices to give your teen. Only give choices which you as a parent can accept. For example, if your teen continues to forget to put his dishes in the dishwasher, a choice might be:

"Either put your dishes in the dishwasher, or I'll leave them in the sink and there will be no clean dishes."

However, if you know that a sink of dirty dishes will drive *you* crazy, then don't give him this choice. Why? Because you will likely sabotage the consequences by getting angry at him as the dishes pile up. In addition, your own values and likes are important. It is much better to keep thinking until you can come up with a consequence that won't punish you. For example:

"Either put your dirty dishes in the dishwasher, or I will serve the next meal without dishes."

By the way, parents who have used the above consequence swear that it takes only one meal of spaghetti eaten off a bare table by hand to teach the lesson. However, once again, if *you* couldn't live with the mess, then don't give this particular choice. What works for one family may not be acceptable for another.

5. Keep your tone firm and calm.

When giving the choice, as well as later when you enforce the consequence, it is essential that you remain both calm and firm. An angry tone of voice (the autocratic parent's pitfall) invites rebellion and a fight. On the other hand, a wishy-washy tone of voice (the permissive parent's pitfall) suggests to the teen that you don't really mean what you say, and also invites rebellion. In a democratic society, a firm and calm tone by an authority figure says, "Hey, I recognize that we are equals and I will treat you respectfully, but you are out of bounds here. My job is to help you learn to stay in bounds, and I plan to do my job."

6. Give the choice one time, then act.

For a logical consequence to teach a lesson, it must be enforced. If the teen continues to choose the negative approach (the misbehavior), then immediately follow through with the consequences. Teens always choose. Even if they don't respond verbally, their behavior will tell you what choice has been made. Do not give the choice a second time without putting the consequences into effect. The teen must see that the choice results in a consequence, and the lesson must be clear, or the value is diminished. For example:

Michael has been given the choice of either leaving parties in which alcohol or other drugs are available or losing the privilege of going to parties for a month. His parents "drop in" at a Saturday night party where Michael has gone, and discover that some of the teenagers are drinking beer. They pull Michael aside and tell him to say his "goodbyes" and come home immediately. They then inform the parents of the teen giving the party about the drinking. When they get home, they talk to Michael about the situation...calmly and firmly. They also let him know that...

"We appreciate the fact that you showed the good judgment not to be drinking yourself. However, since our agreement is that you will also leave such parties on your own, and you chose to stay, there will be no more parties for you for a month."

7. Expect testing.

When you attempt to redirect a teen's misbehavior from negative choices towards positive ones, expect her to continue to misbehave for awhile. We call this testing, because the teen is actually testing to see if we will really do what we say we will do. In other words, will we change *our* behavior? For better or for worse, she was getting some pay-off out of our old way of responding, and she will try to get us to go back to that approach. However, if we will consistently enforce the consequences, she will soon see that her testing isn't working, and change. After all, teens don't do what doesn't work.

8. Allow the teen to try again after experiencing the consequences.

Since the goal is for the teen to learn from the consequences of his choice, then opportunities must be provided to try again. But only after the teen has experienced the consequences of the first choice.

For example, Tom has agreed that *when* he has mowed the lawn, *then* he may go to the swimming pool on Saturdays. Dad sees Tom heading to the pool before the lawn is mowed, and he reminds him of his obligation. After Tom has finished, Dad says,

"I see you have decided to go swimming after all." (Said with a smile.)

If the teen repeats the misbehavior after experiencing the consequences, then he or she is testing. One can meet this challenge by letting the consequences operate a little longer after the second try, and longer yet after the third. For example, if

Tom starts for the swimming pool again next week without mowing the lawn, Dad can say,

"It seems that you have decided not to swim today. We can try again tomorrow."

Logical Consequences Guidelines

1. Give the teen a choice.
   - ■ either/or choice
   - ■ when/then choice
2. Involve the teen in setting the consequence.
3. Make sure the consequence is logical.
4. Give choices that you can live with.
5. Keep your tone firm and calm.
6. Give the choice one time, then act.
7. Expect testing.
8. Allow the teen to try again later.

Parenting and Anger

Anger and its expression have long been a subject of conflict for parents and psychologists alike. Anger seems to be natural, and yet it is often so destructive that we are not quite sure what to make of it. Perhaps these pages will give you a new slant on an old subject.

What Does Anger Mean?

■ **Response to frustration.** Anger is an emotional and physiological response to frustration. If an important need, want or desire is blocked for us, our bodies and our emotions react by being angry.

For example: A caveman, walking through the woods, comes upon a fallen tree which is blocking his path. On the other side of the tree are some berries which he wants to pick and eat. He strains to push the fallen tree aside, but he isn't strong enough, and he becomes frustrated at the thought of not reaching his goal. His frustration produces a whole syndrome of physiological responses which enable him to lift the fallen tree savagely and hurl it aside.

- Purpose of anger. Anger has both physiological and emotional purposes.

  Physiologically, anger releases certain chemicals into our bloodstream; these chemicals produce changes that make us stronger, faster and visually intimidating. This added power may help us remove whatever block is frustrating us. Emotionally, anger often helps us to overcome our inhibitions; it propels us into action which we might not take when we are calmer.

- Old brain-new brain. Anger is associated with the so-called "old brain": that part of the brain that has been present in human beings for millions of years. But as man's new brain evolved in the cerebral cortex that came to surround the old brain, so did man's intelligence. This gives us the means to analyze frustrations and to handle them in other ways than with brute force.

- "Use," not "lose" our temper. Rudolf Dreikurs once said that people do not "lose" their temper; they "use" their temper, just as the caveman did, to remove frustration. We can "use" our temper in positive ways to solve problems.

  Human intelligence is an incredibly effective problem-solver. We have billions of electro-chemical neurons and enough connecting cable to stretch to the moon and back. So we have the resources; we only need to know how to use them.

The Uses of Anger

- The message of anger. Our own angry feelings tell us that one of our goals is being thwarted. They also clearly send this message:

  "Act! Don't just sit there; get up and do something."

  If we do act early, we can take corrective action before the problem gets worse, and before we blow up in a rage.

  If we don't act, but try to ignore the message, then several things could happen:

  1. The problem might go away by other means, but this is risky and uncertain.

2. Our anger will grow in intensity until it propels us into some action, which is likely to be desperate and unthinking.

3. Our anger will seethe internally, expressing itself in unexpected ways: in headaches, rashes, ulcers, even heart attacks.

■ How to act on anger. We can act in three ways when dealing with anger:

1. Act to change the situation:

Example: Struggle until you remove the fallen tree.
Example: Send an "I" Message.

2. Reduce the importance of the goal; put it in perspective (change your thinking):

Example: Although you may want the berries very much, be aware that you don't need them for either your survival or satisfaction.

Example: When a teen insists on giving up music lessons, the parent can remind himself or herself that the goal of playing an instrument is less important than the good relationship with the teen.

3. Change your goals; find an alternative (again, change your thinking):

Example: Decide you don't really care that much about berries, or find an alternative that will satisfy your need...an apple tree near the river.

Example: The parent can give up his goal of having his son play football; encourage an alternative activity of the teen's choice.

Helping Teens Use Their Anger

Because teens are sometimes more primitive in their expression of emotions, they will often resemble the caveman when experiencing frustration and anger. Though tantrums and hitting are more common with young children, teens can also fly off the handle.

How parents can help:

1. By giving them a good model. The way parents handle their own problems and frustrations will provide a model for their teens.

- Does the parent fly into a rage, hurling insults and humiliation?

- Does the parent strike out at others?

- Does the parent sink into a depression (an adult temper tantrum or "silent storm")?

2. By guiding them with words to more effective forms of expression. Example: "You have the right to feel the way you do, but in our family, we don't scream and blame; we look for solutions."

Example: "I can see that you are angry. But tell me with words instead of damaging things."

Example: "When you get angry at me, please tell me without calling me names. I don't call you names; please don't call me names."

Take your sails out of their wind.

3. By removing oneself from a power struggle. When teens have tantrums, you can acknowledge their anger, but at the same time "take your sails out of their wind." Rather than trying to overpower the teen, the parent can withdraw instead. This action says to the teen, "I am not intimidated by your show of temper and will not give in, but I won't punish or humiliate you either." The result is that teens who get neither a fight nor their own way after throwing tantrums will usually find more acceptable ways to influence people.

4. By giving the teen a choice. In those situations where a teen's tantrum leads to the destruction of property, he can be given the choice of either expressing his anger respectfully, with words, or paying for the damage.

5. By allowing the teen to influence the parent's decisions. When a person feels powerless to influence leaders, frustration gives way to anger, rebellion and revolution. If teens participate in decisions that concern them, they will be less likely to resort to such unconscious tactics as stomach disorders, headaches and eating problems, to name a few.

Mutual Respect

Respect is an important aspect of all relationships in a society based on equality; its absence erodes the possibility of cooperation, and breeds resentment and hostility. Teaching teens respect is therefore an important goal of Active Parenting.

How do we teach this basic skill? All parents want their teens to show them respect. But as author Bernard Malamud once wrote, "Respect is what you have to have in order to get." The best way to teach respect, then, is to show respect. Dreikurs' concept of "mutual respect" between parent and teen is an idea that many parents have found invaluable.

The best way to teach respect, is to show respect.

Most adults have learned how to show respect towards other adults. Yet it is easy for parents to slip into disrespect when addressing their own teens. Parents humiliate, criticize, nag, belittle, remind, yell, label, name-call and intimidate; parents do for teens what teens could do for themselves; parents put themselves in service to their teens and even allow teens to abuse them (these too are disrespectful); parents don't listen when teens talk, but become furious when teens do the same thing to them. The list goes on.

As you apply the discipline skills from this session, work at catching yourself *before* you act disrespectfully to your teens. Try to catch yourself with a smile, rather than a kick, and then look for a way to express yourself that is consistent with how you would like to be treated. Notice how your teen responds, and how you feel during the exchange.

Who Owns the Problem?

SCENE #1 (Dad's house)

      Who owned the problem?_____

      Why?_____

      _____

SCENE #2 (Gas)

      Who owned the problem?_____

      Why?_____

      _____

SCENE #3 (Curfew)

      Who owned the problem?_____

      Why?_____

      _____

SCENE #4 (Think of a problem from your own family.)

      What happened?_____

      _____

      _____

      Who owned the problem?_____

      Why?_____

      _____

      _____

" I " Messages

Try writing an "I" Message for the following example: Your teenage son has been blasting his stereo for the past 15 minutes and you're getting a terrible headache. You've already asked him politely to turn the stereo down, but somehow the volume has gotten back up. Fill in the following "I" Message as you might express it to your son:

When you_____

I feel _____

because _____

I would like (Will you please) _____

_____

Write down a problem from your own family in which you own the problem. Now write an "I" Message that you can use at home this week to solve the problem:

When you _____

I feel _____

because _____

I would like (Will you please) _____

_____

Evaluation

How did your teen respond to your "I" Message?

_____

_____

What did you like about the way you delivered the "I" Message?

_____

_____

How would you do it differently next time?

_____

_____

_____

_____

Logical Consequences

SCENE	TYPE OF CONSEQUENCE (Logical, Natural, or Punishment)	MISTAKES MADE (If Any)
#1		
#2		
#3		
#4		
#5		

Using Logical Consequences

Using the same problem for which you constructed an "I" Message in Activity III-B, write down a logical consequence you might employ in order to deal with the problem. Write in the space below one way that you might present the choices and consequences to your teen during the discussion of the problem:

_____

_____

_____

If your "I" Message was effective, you didn't get a chance to practice your logical consequence. Think of another problem in which you can develop a logical consequence. Write down the problem here:

_____

_____

_____

Now, write down a choice and a logical consequence that you could use:

_____

_____

_____

Meet with your teen to discuss the problem, and use this logical consequence or one that you developed with the teen.

Evaluation

What was your teen's response to the discussion?

_____

_____

Using Logical Consequences

What was his response to the logical consequence? (Did he test you to see if you would follow through?)

_____

_____

_____

If the consequence isn't working, do you think you need to stick with it longer or change the consequence to something else?

_____

_____

_____

If the consequence isn't working, have you violated any of the guidelines for setting up logical consequences? (Check page 91.)

_____

_____

What do you like about the way you handled the use of logical consequences?

_____

_____

What will you do differently next time?

_____

_____

_____

Prevention Talk

First, review pages 74 to 77 in the *Parent's Guide*. Then, choose a situation in which your teen's behavior might conflict with your expectations and cause a problem (for example, use of the car, dating, spending the night out, being left home alone.):

_____

_____

List the specific aspects of the situation that you and your teen will want to discuss:

_____

_____

After your talk, check which of the seven steps you completed:

	Yes	No
Step 1: Define the problem.	_____	_____
Step 2: Share thoughts and feelings.	_____	_____
Step 3: Brainstorm solutions.	_____	_____
Step 4: Decide through discussion.	_____	_____
Step 5: Decide on logical consequences.	_____	_____
Step 6: Put into action.	_____	_____
Step 7: Follow-up.	_____	_____

What did you like about how your talk went?

_____

_____

What will you do differently next time?

_____

_____

Do you think your talk helped prevent any problems this week? If so, which ones?

_____

_____

If problems occurred, did you follow through with logical consequences? If so, how did it go?

_____

_____

Winning

Cooperation

Through

Communication

Chapter 7

Active
Communication

A slave on a Roman galley was rowing his oar to the beat of the drum. As he methodically did his job, he looked over at the slave next to him. He was horrified at what he saw. The slave in the next seat was drilling a hole in the bottom of the boat under his seat. As the water began to gush into the boat, the first slave exclaimed, "What in Jupiter's name are you doing!?" The second slave replied, "What's it to you? I'm only drilling the hole under *my* seat."

The joke, of course, is that when we are all riding in the same boat, no matter whose seat the hole is under, everyone is going to get wet. Nowhere is this more true than in a family. When one member has a problem, the ripples are felt throughout the family.

Active Parenting of Teens has stressed four main qualities that form the foundation of the individual's ability to succeed in our democratic society: self-esteem, courage, responsibility and cooperation. Cooperation, the gentle art of working together for the common good, is the subject of this chapter.

Communication: The Road to Cooperation

Families and societies that recognize that we are all traveling in the same boat place a tremendous value on cooperation. They know that people will perform better when they have the ability to participate in the decision making process. That none of us is as smart and as capable as all of us. That when people work together cooperatively, amazing things happen: problems are solved and civilizations are built.

Simply stated:

Cooperation is two or more people working toward a common goal.

In a society of equals the teenager who learns how to work cooperatively with others, to be a team player, has a far greater chance of success than the one who overemphasizes competition. Ironically, though the ability to compete is certainly a major part of our society, the ability to cooperate is what makes us great.

One of the best ways to teach cooperation to your teenager is through problem solving. In the last chapter we discussed the role of discipline in handling problems that belong to the parent. Even in those cases, we stressed the importance of including the teen in the problem solving process. When the problem belongs to the teen, we have a unique opportunity to help the teen find a solution. We can do this with good communication skills. We can do this respectfully, and without robbing the teen of the responsibility for deciding how to handle his problem.

Through active communication between you and your teen, an important side effect occurs: the teen learns that "two heads are better than one" — that when we solve problems cooperatively, better solutions are found. This teamwork, and the solutions it often brings, not only fosters a respect for cooperation, it

also strengthens the relationship between parent and teen. And that translates to more satisfaction and harmony for the entire family.

The Problem Handling Model Again

Let's look once again at the model for handling problems in a family. When we presented this model in Session III (see page 72), we focused on the discipline side of parenting (when we own the problem). Now we will look at the support side of parenting (when our teen owns a problem). The skills used for supporting a teen in solving a problem are highlighted in red.

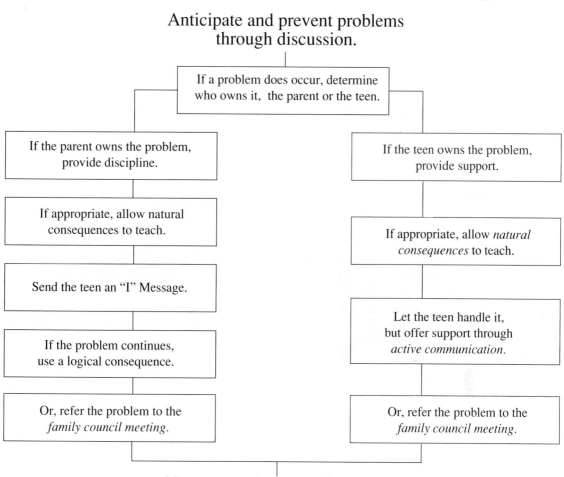

Anticipate and prevent problems
through discussion.

If a problem does occur, determine
who owns it, the parent or the teen.

| If the parent owns the problem, provide discipline. | If the teen owns the problem, provide support. |

If appropriate, allow natural
consequences to teach.

Send the teen an "I" Message.

If appropriate, allow *natural
consequences* to teach.

If the problem continues,
use a logical consequence.

Let the teen handle it,
but offer support through
active communication.

Or, refer the problem to the
family council meeting.

Or, refer the problem to the
family council meeting.

No matter who owns the problem,
offer encouragement.

Avoiding Communication Blocks

Half of good communication is avoiding bad communication. When a teen has a problem, she is particularly sensitive. If she pays us the great compliment of beginning to discuss this problem with us, she is putting her self-esteem at risk. If we say or do something that injures her self-esteem at this point, she will withdraw. In other words, we will have blocked the communication.

A communication block is any remark or attitude on the part of the listener that injures the speaker's self-esteem to the extent that communication is broken off.

Communication blocks are usually a product of disrespect. It is not that we mean the teen any harm; in fact, our intentions are usually to help. However, our attitude demeans the teen in some way. In our society of equals, an individual's self-esteem is very important. We are wary of signs of disrespect, and we are quick to withdraw from those who show us these signs. Yet, we all make these mistakes and block communication. Please look at the chart on page 109 of common parental communication blocks, and try to recognize which ones you use most often.

When a teen runs into communication blocks often enough, the teen eventually decides that this is not a person to trust with a problem. On the positive side, when active communication skills are used, the teen feels comfortable going to the parent with problems, even big ones. The parent then becomes what is sometimes called an "askable parent." When it comes to critical matters such as sexuality, alcohol and other drugs, it pays to have established such a line of communication.

Active Communication

Active communication is a set of communication skills that allows parents to support a teen in handling her own problems. These skills can be learned, and they can be steadily improved with practice. Active communication is called for in situations in which the teen owns the problem, or in which the teen and the parent share responsibility for the problem. There are five skills involved. They are:

1. LISTEN ACTIVELY.

2. LISTEN FOR FEELINGS.

3. CONNECT FEELINGS TO CONTENT.

4. LOOK FOR ALTERNATIVES AND PREDICT CONSEQUENCES.

5. FOLLOW UP.

Communication Blocks

Communication block	Parent's intention	Why it's disrespectful	Examples
Commanding	To control the situation and provide teen with quick solutions.	It says to the teen, "You don't have the right to decide how to handle your own problems."	"What you should do is...." "Stop complaining."
Giving Advice	To influence the teen with arguments or opinions.	It says to the teen, "You don't have the good sense to come up with your own solutions."	"I've got a good idea...." "Why don't you...."
Placating	To take away the teen's pain; to make her feel better.	It says to the teen, "You don't have a right to your feelings; you can't handle discomfort."	"It isn't as bad as it seems." "Everything will be okay."
Interrogating	To get to the bottom of the problem and find out what the teen did wrong.	It says to the teen, "You must have messed up somewhere."	"What did you do to make him...?"
Distracting	To protect the teen from the problem by changing the subject.	It says to the teen, "I don't think you can stand the discomfort long enough to find a real solution."	"Let's not worry about that, let's...."
Psychologizing	To help prevent future problems by analyzing the teen's behavior and explaining his motives.	It says to the teen, "I know more about you than you know about yourself. Therefore, I'm superior to you."	"Do you know why you said that?" "You're just insecure."
Sarcasm	To show the teen how wrong her attitudes or behavior are by making her feel ridiculous.	It says to the teen, "You are ridiculous."	"Well, I guess that's just about the end of the world."
Moralizing	To show the teen the proper way to deal with the problem.	It says to the teen, "Don't you dare choose your own values."	"The right thing to do would be to...." "Oh, how awful."
Know-It-All	To show the teen that he has a resource for handling any problem; namely, the parent.	It says to the teen, "Since I know it all, you must know nothing."	"The solution is really very simple...."

1. Listen Actively

Keeping in mind the need to avoid communication blocks, let's move on to the first step in active communication: active listening. Why do we say active listening? Because if you listen fully, you are not just a passive receiver of information; you are an active participant in the communication process. You listen with your eyes as well as your ears; with your intuition as well as your thinking abilities. Your object in listening actively is to encourage the teen to express what he is thinking and feeling.

Listen with your eyes as well as your ears.

- **Keep your own talk to a minimum.** You are not listening when you are talking. When you are actively listening to a teen, your role is to listen, not talk.

- **Give full attention.** When parents are listening actively, they give their full attention to the teen and what he is saying. When parents give their full attention, the teen will usually feel encouraged by the attention alone. The attention says, "I care about you; you matter; I'm here to help."

- **Acknowledge what you are hearing.** Active listening is not characterized by absolute silence on the part of the listener. When listening to a teen, it helps to show that you are understanding, that you are taking it in. You can say something as simple as "I see" now and then, or even "Umm-hmm." You can ask questions that clarify what the teen is saying, or you can summarize lengthy or complicated stories.

2. Listen for Feelings

There are no wrong feelings, for either parents or teens. There are certainly unpleasant feelings, and they often suggest mistaken attitudes or perceptions, but feelings in themselves are not wrong or right. They simply are, and whether we like it or not, they influence us. In fact, they influence us more when we don't acknowledge and accept them. Acknowledging and accepting our feelings doesn't necessarily mean that we act on them, but only that we look at the feelings to see what information they can give us about our own response to a given situation or problem.

Acknowledging our feelings is often a first step in dealing with a problem.

So, acknowledging our feelings surrounding a problem is often a first step in dealing with that problem. Parents can help teens learn to acknowledge their own feelings by listening for the feelings implied in what they say. Sometimes the teen is unaware of the feeling, but when the parent names the feeling for him, the teen sees the truth.

3. Connect Feelings to Content

When a parent has actively listened to the content of what a teen has to say, and has an idea of what the teen is feeling, the next step is to reflect those feelings back to the teen. The parent becomes what psychologist Haim Ginott called an "emotional mirror," so that the teen can connect the feelings with the content of his or her problem.

This "reflection" takes the form of a tentative statement like this:

> *"It sounds as though you might be resentful that Lonnie's score was better than yours."*

4. Look for Alternatives/Predict Consequences

Helping a teen become an effective problem solver means helping him learn to look at alternative solutions and weigh the potential consequences. Many times, merely helping the teen to connect feeling and content is enough to suggest a solution. However, some problems are more difficult to deal with than others, and they require some action to remedy the situation. In many cases a parent can begin by encouraging the teen to look at the possible alternatives:

> *"What can you do about that?"*

> *"What else can you try?"*

After each alternative, the parent can help the child predict the consequences of that alternative:

> *"What do you think would happen if you did that?"*

It is better for the teen to think of alternatives on her own, without prompting. If the teen cannot think of any, the parent can tentatively suggest some. Also, it can be helpful for a parent to share a personal experience in a similar situation, so long as he or she doesn't use the testimonial as a weapon, urging a specific course of action on the teen. You could say something like:

> *"I don't know what you will decide to do, but I remember a time when a friend of mine named Anita moved away without even saying goodbye. I felt hurt, then angry, then sad...."*

The choice must be the teen's if she is to learn responsibility.

It is important to let the teen have final responsibility for deciding which alternative she will choose. Refrain from telling the teen what to do. The choice must be the teen's if she is to learn responsibility. When a teen figures out what to do, she feels a sense of self-esteem and she accepts responsibility for her choices.

5. Follow Up

Before letting go of the problem, there is one final step: seeking some kind of commitment from the teen to take a course of action. In other words, ask the teen what he intends to do, and when. This can be done gently, with an understanding that even Einstein often needed some time to let new information incubate before his course of action became clear.

After the teen has had an opportunity to handle the problem, follow up by beginning the active communication process over again:

"How did it go with...?"

In doing so, the parent not only helps the teen make sense of the total experience, but also confirms to him that the interest was genuine.

WHAT THE TEEN SAYS	FEELING WORD	WHAT THE PARENT SAYS
Mom, I'm not going to clean my dumb room!	Angry	You're angry that I want you to clean up your room.
I missed the foul shot, and we lost the game.	Disappointed	Sounds like you're disappointed about missing the shot.
I don't like to smile. I hate these braces.	Embarrassed	You're embarrassed to smile with braces on your teeth.

Feeling Words

Although the English language has hundreds of words that describe specific feelings, most people do not have many on the tip of their tongue. As you practice looking for the right "feeling words," you will find that your feeling word vocabulary increases and the job gets easier. To help with this process, we have included a list of 100 common feeling words for you to keep in mind.

WORDS THAT DESCRIBE PLEASANT FEELINGS		WORDS THAT DESCRIBE UNPLEASANT FEELINGS	
accepted	hopeful	afraid	jealous
adequate	humble	angry	let down
adventurous	important	anxious	lonely
bold	joyful	ashamed	miserable
brilliant	lovely	bashful	nervous
calm	loving	bored	overwhelmed
caring	overjoyed	cautious	pained
cheered	peaceful	cheated	possessive
comfortable	peppy	concerned	provoked
confident	playful	defeated	pushed
content	pleased	defiant	rejected
daring	proud	disappointed	remorseful
eager	refreshed	discouraged	resentful
elated	relieved	down	shy
encouraged	satisfied	embarrassed	stupid
energetic	secure	envious	suspicious
excited	snappy	foolish	tired
fascinated	successful	frustrated	trapped
free	surprised	guilty	uncomfortable
full	sympathetic	hateful	uneasy
glad	tranquil	hesitant	unhappy
great	understood	hopeless	unloved
gutsy	warm	hurt	unsure
happy	wonderful	impatient	weary
high	zany	irritated	worried

Putting Active Communication
to Work

Now that you are aware of the five steps of the active communication process, begin looking for opportunities to use them in supporting your teen in finding solutions to problems. You'll find that the more supportive you are, the more cooperative your teen is likely to become.

However, if your relationship is still characterized by power struggles, disrespect or animosity, then your teen may not be willing yet to sit down for a lengthy discussion. You can still use what you have learned to begin winning his cooperation by listening for his feelings, and expressing empathy.

For example: *"Boy, you sure look down."*

"I guess you're really ticked off."

"That must have really hurt."

You can even use this skill when disciplining your teen or denying him permission to do something; it will help reduce his anger. Just having his feelings recognized and accepted can sometimes help.

For example: *"I know you're angry that I won't let you go."*

"If looks could kill, I'd be in real trouble right now."

"I can live with you hating me right now, but I don't think I could live with hating myself if I let you do something I knew was dangerous, and something terrible happened to you."

Family Enrichment Activity #4

Expressing Love

Building a positive relationship with teenagers is an ongoing process, and it sometimes takes steady effort. As we have seen earlier, it involves making arrangements to have fun together, teaching specific skills to teenagers, and mutual respect. But the positive relationship between parent and teen involves, most of all, expressing love for each other. All teenagers hunger for love, even those who make a career of acting unlovable. Teenagers need to know that whatever else may happen, their parents love them. Methods of expressing love to teens can be woven into the fabric of everyday life: a kiss, a pat on the back, a tousling of hair, an arm around the shoulder. But it is equally important for a parent to be able to say to a teen that you love him or her. The words may come awkwardly for some parents. But the important thing is how beautiful they sound to all teens!

Teenagers need to know that whatever else may happen, their parents love them.

Parents can say "I love you" at an unexpected time when the teen will be surprised at the timing, but pleased with the message. Parents can say "I love you" at a time of calmness or tenderness, such as bedtime, and the teen can bask in the warmth of the words. Parents can even say "I love you" as a nonsensical answer to a teen's question, if they want to get the message across without being too serious about it:

"Dad, how do you spell 'apparent'?"

"I-L-O-V-E-Y-O-U."

"Oh? Who taught you to spell?"

"You and Mom."

"I love you, too. Now, how do you *really* spell 'apparent'?"

Your assignment this week is to find ways to express your love to each of your teens, with at least one verbal expression of love.

Chapter 8

The Family Council Meeting

The family council meeting offers an ideal forum in which all family members participate in resolving family problems and making family decisions.

One of the themes stressed in Active Parenting is the importance of allowing teenagers a voice in decisions that affect their lives. Just as freedom of speech is the basic freedom in our democratic society, a cooperative household must allow its members the same freedom. Of course, democracy doesn't mean that you will always get your way, it means that you will always get your say. By allowing teenagers to influence our decisions through respectful discussion, we are better able to maintain our parental authority.

The feeling on the part of teens that their voices and opinions make a difference builds cooperation and responsibility, and at the same time it makes anger and rebellion less likely. The family council meeting offers an ideal forum in which all family members participate in resolving family problems and making family decisions.

Simply stated, the family council meeting is a time, once a week, when the entire family gathers to make plans and handle problems that affect family members. It can last anywhere from 20 minutes to an hour, and is conducted according to an agenda. It is in effect what a business meeting is to an organization, only less boring because, after all, everything on the agenda "hits home."

Six Good Reasons for Holding a Family Council Meeting

1. Cooperation: Regular family meetings teach each person in the family that all are in the same boat, that all on board can share in steering the boat, and that the best way to decide how and where to steer it is to share feelings and opinions until an agreement is reached.

2. Responsibility: The regular participation in family meetings teaches each person in the family that he or she, together with the other family members, must make the best choices they can make on behalf of the family; after all, everyone will have to live with the consequences once the choices are made.

3. Courage: The family meeting is a laboratory for individual courage. Each family member learns how important it is to say what he or she really thinks and feels, even if it isn't shared by anybody else. The agenda also provides a specific opportunity for sharing encouragement.

4. Love: The family meeting lets love flow within the family circle, as family members share their feelings honestly with each other.

5. Unity: The family meeting is living proof that the family is a single body, tied together not only by kinship and daily association, but also by common purposes and a common way of dealing with problems and decisions.

6. Education: The family meeting teaches children a way of being in the world. Each family is a miniature society, and the social skills and attitudes which children develop within the family circle are the skills and attitudes which they will carry with them into the adult world. This is a place to teach democratic principles.

How to Get Started with Family Council Meetings

■ **Parental initiative.** Parents are usually the ones to present the idea of having family meetings, and to get the meetings started. Here are some points for parents to consider in setting up a family council meeting.

■ **Start with those who are willing to attend.** It happens sometimes that some family members are not ready to discuss matters in a family meeting, or they feel that the idea is not a good one. But this doesn't mean that the idea should be abandoned. Family meetings can still be held, if most family members agree on holding them. Those who do not attend the early meetings may decide to attend later when they see the advantages.

Anyone who has a stake in decisions affecting the daily life of the family should be present.

■ **Who should attend family meetings?** Family meetings should include parents, children and any others who live with the family, such as grandparents, uncles or aunts. In other words, anyone who has a stake in decisions affecting the daily life of the family should be present.

■ **Single-parent households.** Families affected by separation or divorce can still hold family meetings, even though one parent will not be participating. In those cases it is important for the family to avoid discussing matters pertaining to the children's relationship with the absent parent. Those matters are owned by the children and the absent parent; if there are problems, they should be handled by active communication, away from the family meeting.

■ **Time and place.** Select a time and a place which is convenient and agreeable to everyone who will be attending. A good time for family meetings is Sunday afternoons, the beginning of the week. The family is more likely to

be together at that time, and the past week can be reviewed, the forthcoming week anticipated. The meetings should be held in a place which is comfortable for all participants, preferably around a large table with enough room for everyone to pull up a chair.

■ **The first meeting.** The first family meeting should be a short one. It's an excellent idea to have only one item of business at this meeting: to plan an outing or a time for fun together right after the meeting. Later meetings can be longer, and follow a more extensive agenda.

Leadership Roles

There are two leadership roles at family meetings:

> 1. Chairperson, who keeps the discussion on track and sees that everybody's opinion is heard, and

> 2. Secretary, who takes notes during the meeting, writes up the minutes after the meeting, and reads the minutes at the next meeting.

These two duties can be assumed by the parents at the first meeting. After that, other family members should take turns at being Chairperson and Secretary in an agreed-upon order, so that no one person is in charge every time.

Overall Agenda

Here is an agenda which works for many families. You can modify it to fit your circumstances.

1. Compliments: This is the time for family members to say "thanks" to each other for good deeds done or for help given during the past week, and to acknowledge strengths and encourage improvement.

2. Minutes: Last week's Secretary reads the minutes for the last meeting.

3. Old Business: Topics unfinished at the last meeting can be discussed further.

4. Finances: Many families have a special item for discussing financial matters. This is also a good time to pass out allowances.

5. New Business: Discussion of new topics, complaints or problems on the agenda.

6. Treat: The meeting adjourns, but the family stays together for a game, an outing or a dessert. This provides an opportunity to have fun together, to enjoy each other's company, and get the week off to a good start.

New Business Agenda

Most families find that the new business section of the family meeting works better if items have been written on a posted agenda before the meeting. A sheet of paper labeled "The Agenda" can be taped to the refrigerator or posted at another convenient location. When a problem occurs that a family member would like handled at the next family meeting, he or she writes it on the agenda. For example:

The Agenda

1. Megan comes into my room without knocking (Ty).
2. Raising allowances (Megan).
3. Planning for the holidays (Mom).

Agenda items are handled in order at the next family meeting. Items that are not brought up before the meeting time is over can be carried over to the next meeting. Many times, an agenda item will have been handled by those involved before the meeting, and can be dropped from the list.

One final benefit of having a written agenda is that it offers parents an excellent way of staying out of children's fights. When a child tries to engage you in solving one of his or her problems, you can sympathetically suggest that it be put on the agenda for this week's meeting. For example:

Ty: "Megan keeps coming into my room without knocking.
       Tell her to stop."

Mother: "Gee, honey, you sound pretty angry about that. Why
        don't you put it on the agenda for this week's family meeting?"

Some Ground Rules for Conducting
Family Council Meetings

■   **Every person has an equal voice.** Although it is hard for parents to
     give up some of their authority, family meetings don't work well unless
     every person has an equal voice in the decisions made. Every person,
     including small children, needs to feel that he or she will be heard, and can
     make a difference in what the family decides to do. Children will not be
     very enthusiastic about family meetings, nor will they derive much benefit
     from them, if the meetings are merely forums for parents to decide what
     everybody will do.

■   **Everyone may share what he or she thinks and feels about each issue.**
     It is important that every person at family meetings be encouraged to speak
     up and say what he or she thinks and feels about whatever question is on
     the table. In order to make decisions that are reasonable and fair to
     everyone, the family needs to hear what all the opinions and feelings are,
     even the negative ones.

■   **Decisions are made by consensus.** Reaching a consensus means that
     when there is disagreement, the parties involved discuss the matter until
     everyone agrees. It does not mean that a vote is taken and the majority
     rules. If an agreement cannot be reached in a family meeting, then one of
     two things may happen: either the matter is tabled until the next meeting
     when it will be discussed further, or (if it urgently requires decision and
     action) the parent may exercise his or her duty as head of the household to
     make a decision and carry it out.

■   **All decisions hold until the next meeting.** Whatever decisions are made
     at a family meeting, they should be carried out at least until the next
     meeting, when they can be discussed again. Complaints after the meeting
     about decisions made should always bring this rejoinder: "Bring it up again
     at the next family meeting."

■ **Some decisions are reserved for parents to make.** Meeting together does not imply that the parents must always do whatever the children decide to do. Basic questions of health and welfare are parental responsibilities, and the decision is sometimes theirs alone to make. But discussion should always be allowed and encouraged. Sometimes a parent must tell the children of a decision already made. When a parent has been told by his or her company that a move is required, for example, he or she can't ask the children for approval. However, the parent can allow them to express their thoughts, concerns and feelings about the move, and to share in the planning.

How to Handle Problems in a Group

■ **Define the problem.** The person with the complaint or the issue to raise is asked to explain it. He or she should always be asked, "Is this still a problem?" If it is still a problem, the person can be simply asked, "What happened?"

■ **Clarify the problem with active listening.** Persons in the group ask clarifying questions, and reflect back to the complainer what he or she is saying. At the end of this process, the Chairperson should get agreement about the problem. For example, "So we all agree, don't we, that Susan borrowed Jason's tennis racquet without asking, and it was stolen?" This is the time for family members to share thoughts and feelings about the problem.

■ **Generate possible solutions through brainstorming.** In "brainstorming" members think of all the possible solutions to a problem, no matter how silly or impractical the solutions may seem. This process is important because ideas generate other ideas; one person's silly idea may contain the germ of a practical solution. To keep the ideas flowing, no one is allowed at this point to say whether the ideas are good or bad; they are simply tossed out into the group without evaluation. The Secretary lists them on paper until no further ideas are forthcoming. Then each idea is discussed.

■ **Arrive at a decision through discussion.** Every person now has a chance

to say what he or she thinks and feels about each possible solution. Those ideas which are not acceptable to most people are discarded, and discussion centers on one or two ideas which are thought to be plausible. Discussion continues until all people in the group agree on one solution.

- **Put the decision into action.** The solution arrived at by brainstorming and discussion is put into effect. In family meetings the solution remains in effect until the next family meeting, when it can be re-evaluated and modified.

How to Be an Effective Chairperson

Just follow the agenda:

1. Compliments: Ask who wants to say that they appreciate the words or the actions of someone during the past week. This is a time for members of the family to say thanks to each other for good deeds, and to encourage each other with compliments.

2. Minutes: First ask the person who was Secretary last week to read the minutes aloud. The minutes remind everyone of what happened at the last meeting.

3. Old business: Ask the family to talk about any matter that wasn't finished at the last meeting. These unfinished matters are called "old business." Let each person say what he or she wants to say, but remind people that they should not talk when someone else is talking.

4. Finances: This is the time for members to bring up matters concerning the "family bank." Ask, "Does anyone have any financial matters?" After the family handles these matters, ask Mom or Dad to pass out allowances.

5. New business: Next, ask the family to talk about matters that have been written on The Agenda. You should read "How to Handle Problems in Groups" on page 122, to learn a good method of solving problems that may come up.

6. Adjourn to a treat: End the meeting by saying, "The meeting is adjourned." People get tired if meetings go on too long, so keep your meeting to the agreed-upon time limit. Usually, your family will have a game or a dessert after the meeting so that you can end on a positive note.

How to Be an Effective Secretary

A guide for family members: To be an effective Secretary, you need to do only three things:

1. Listen carefully to what is said.

2. Write down what is decided on each matter that is talked about.

3. Later (after the meeting) write a summary of what was decided. This summary is called "the minutes." Read the minutes aloud at the next meeting.

Here is what the minutes may look like:

Minutes of family meeting, March 14, 19__.

Chairperson was Jerry. Secretary was Linda.

The family decided that:

1. We would go to Colorado this summer for vacation.

2. Jerry will pay Linda $5 out of his allowance for the lost cassette tape.

3. We will wait until the next meeting to decide whether we want to go on the weekend hike in April with the Sierra Club.

Communication Block Exercise

We all tend to use communication blocks at one time or another. Or, as one parent put it, "My skill is such that I can use three or four of these blocks at one time." To catch ourselves before we block communication, it helps to know what our individual pitfalls are.

Think about the communication blocks that you tend to use most often. Write this in the block below. Then indicate the situations that usually bring them out, and what you see as your intention for using that block.

BLOCK	SITUATION	INTENTION
Example: Distracting	Son didn't make football team.	To reduce my own bad feelings about his bad feelings.

Connecting Feelings to Content

SCENE	TEEN'S FEELING	PARENT'S RESPONSE
#1 (Ty)		
#2 (Tonya)		
#3 (José)		
#4 (Megan)		
#5 (José)		
#6 (Ty)		
#7 (Megan)		
#8 (Ty's friend)		
#9 (Ty)		
#10 (José)		

Active Communication Evaluation

After you've had a chance to practice your active communication skills with one of your teens this week, fill out the following evaluation so that you can be sure to learn from the experience.

What was the situation or problem that you talked to your teen about?

_____

_____

How did you approach your teen?

_____

_____

List examples of the five steps of active communication that you were able to use:

       1) Listen actively _____

       2) Listen for feelings _____

       3) Connect feelings to content _____

       4) Look for alternatives and predict consequences _____

       5) Follow up_____

How did your teen respond to your effort?

_____

What did you like about how you handled the process?

_____

What would you do differently next time?

_____

_____

Expressing Love

Remember When

Think back once again to when you were a teen, and recall a time when an adult in your life expressed love to you. Maybe it was a parent; maybe a grandparent, another relative or a friend. Maybe the expression was verbal; maybe it was nonverbal.

Describe the experience:

_____

_____

How did you feel?

_____

_____

Expressing love at home

To help you remember your expressions of love to your teen or teens, fill in the following chart:

CHILD'S NAME	YOUR EXPRESSION	YOUR CHILD'S RESPONSE

Family Council Evaluation

Like any new skill, holding a family council meeting is likely to feel a bit awkward the first time you try it. To help you learn from your first experience this week, fill in the following evaluation after your family council meeting.

How did you introduce the idea of a family meeting to your teens?

_____

_____

How did they respond?

_____

_____

How were you able to enlist their cooperation? (If you were unsuccessful, what happened?)

_____

_____

What were the positives in the meeting?

_____

_____

What were the problems?

_____

_____

What did you like about how you handled the meeting?

_____

_____

What will you do differently next time?

_____

_____

HOW TO SAY "NO"
WITHOUT LOOKING
LIKE A JERK

1) Ask questions.
2) Name the trouble.
3) Identify the consequences
4) Suggest an alternative.
5) Walk and talk leaving
   the door open.

The Challenge
of Alcohol and
Other Drugs

Chapter 9

Drugs and Teens: A Bad Mix

On Saturday afternoon about 1 p.m., 13-year-old David met up with some buddies to go to the playground to play basketball. On the way one of them pulled out a brown paper bag, unscrewed the top of the enclosed bottle, and took a short swig of 80 proof whiskey. Without a word he passed the bottle to the guy next to him who also took a swig. As the bottle moved from teen to teen, the pressure on David mounted. He didn't want to drink, but he didn't want to look ridiculous either. And he certainly didn't want to be left out of the group.

On Saturday night at 11:30, 16-year-old Rhonda was at a party at a friend's house. The friend's parents, not wanting to intrude, were upstairs watching television. Some of the kids were out in their cars drinking beer. Two of Rhonda's best friends pulled her into the bathroom and locked the door. "You've got to try this," said one, as she carefully poured a small amount of white powder onto the counter top. "This coke is the best," said the other, as the lines of cocaine were neatly formed with a razor blade. "I don't know," said Rhonda.

The Problem

Every day thousands of teenagers are offered a chance to try alcohol or other drugs. And their parents aren't around to tell them not to. Every day thousands of teenagers give in to the pressure to try alcohol or other drugs. Many go on to become regular users. Some become addicts. Some become overdose victims. To quote California Attorney General John Van Kemp, "It is a sad and sobering reality that trying drugs is no longer the exception among high school students, it is the norm."

Some of the facts that make drug use the single greatest challenge facing us as parents:

■   A Gallup survey reported that when 13- to 18-year-olds were asked to name the biggest problem facing young people today, drugs topped the list.

■   The U.S. has the highest rate of teenage drug use of any industrialized nation (for example, 10 times as great as Japan's).

■   61% of high school seniors have used drugs other than alcohol.

■   41% of high school seniors reported using marijuana in the last year; 26% in the last month.

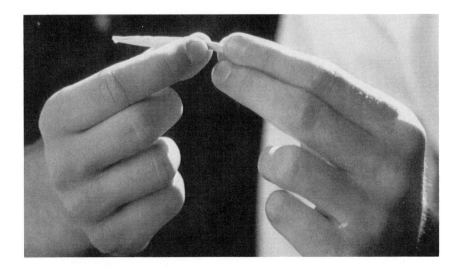

- 13% of high school seniors reported using cocaine in the past year (up 100% from the last decade).

- Initial drug use occurs at an increasingly early age. The percentage of sixth graders using drugs has tripled over the last decade.

- Research shows that drug use among teens is 10 times as prevalent as parents suspect.

- Drug use is not confined to certain population groups or economic levels; it affects our entire society.

- All drug use is dangerous. There is no such thing as safe or responsible use of illegal drugs.

Alcohol and Other Drugs Are Clearly Harmful to Teens

Research on the use of alcohol and other drugs (including nicotine) by teenagers overwhelmingly points out the negative effects. Although many parents can remember their own teenage experimentations, it is unwise to assume that because they came out undamaged their teens will be as fortunate. The risks

involved in using drugs today are much greater:

- The marijuana used today is 5-20 times as strong as that used as recently as the mid-70s.

- Recent research indicates that teenagers who drink are much more susceptible to alcoholism than adults.

- New, so-called "designer" drugs, synthetic variations on existing illegal drugs, have been known to cause permanent brain damage with a single dose.

- Phencyclidine (PCP), first developed as an animal tranquilizer, has unpredictable and often violent effects. Teens are often unaware that they are using this dangerous drug when PCP-laced parsley in cigarette form is passed off as marijuana, or when PCP in crystal form is sold as lysergic acid (LSD).

- Cocaine, especially in its newer crystal form called "crack," is more available than ever before. It is highly addictive and can be deadly.

How Alcohol and Other Drugs
Can Hurt Your Teen

Teens are particularly vulnerable to alcohol and other drugs because they affect normal development in a number of ways:

- They can interfere with memory, sensation and perception.

- They distort experiences and can lead to a loss of self-control that can cause users to harm themselves and others.

- They interfere with the brain's ability to take in, sort and synthesize information. The ability to understand information is blocked or distorted.

- They can give a distorted view of functioning. For example, an intoxicated teen driving home from a party may think that he is driving as well as a professional race car driver, when in fact he has lost much of his ability to react quickly or perceive accurately.

Physical effects:

- Physical dependence. The body begins to crave the drug, and violent withdrawal symptoms occur if use is stopped.

- Tolerance. Over time, larger doses of the drug must be used to attain the same "high." Teens often respond by combining drugs, often with disastrous results.

- Flashbacks. Fat-soluble drugs such as marijuana, PCP and LSD seek out and settle in the body's fatty tissues, such as those in the brain. Such accumulation of drugs and their slow release over time may cause delayed effects (flashbacks) weeks and even months after drug use has stopped.

Psychological and social effects:

- Psychological dependence. This occurs when drug taking becomes the center of the user's life.

- Erosion of school performance.

- Destruction of ties to family, friends, outside interests, values and goals.

- Shift from taking drugs to feel good, to taking drugs to keep from feeling bad.

- Suicidal feeling. Over half of all teen suicides are drug-related.

Crack: A Nightmare on Elm Street

Cocaine use is the fastest-growing drug problem in America.

Although all illegal drugs, including alcohol, pose a serious threat, cocaine use is the fastest-growing drug problem in America. Most alarming is the availability of cocaine in a cheap but potent form called crack or rock. Crack is a purified form of cocaine that is smoked. There are five reasons that it has become a major problem throughout the country, from Broadway to Elm Street:

1. Crack is inexpensive to try. Available for as little as $10, crack is affordable to many new users, including teens and even preteens.

2. Crack is easy to use. It is sold in pieces resembling small white gravel or soap chips, and is sometimes pressed into small white pellets. Crack can be smoked in a pipe or put into cigarettes. Because the visible effects disappear within minutes after smoking, it can be used almost anytime during the day.

3. Crack is extremely addictive. It is far more addictive than heroin or barbiturates. Because crack is smoked, it is quickly absorbed into the bloodstream. It produces a feeling of extreme euphoria, peaking within seconds. The desire to repeat this sensation can cause addiction within days.

4. Crack leads to crime and severe psychological disorders. Many youths, once addicted, have turned to stealing, prostitution and drug dealing to support their habit. Continued use can produce violent behavior and psychotic behavior similar to schizophrenia.

5. Crack is deadly. Cocaine in any form can cause cardiac arrest and death by interrupting the brain's control over the heart and respiratory system.

Why Teens Become Harmfully Involved with Drugs

A teen or preteen may begin experimenting with alcohol and other drugs for a number of reasons. In fact, drugs offer a negative means of achieving any of the five basic goals described in Chapter 2: contact, power, protection, withdrawal, challenge. As we look more closely at the negative approaches to these basic goals, keep in mind that the negative approach is usually the result of low self-esteem and discouragement.

Contact

Because teens have a heightened desire to belong, they are very susceptible to peer pressure. The first temptations to use drugs often come in social situations in the form of pressure to "act grown up" and "have a good time" by smoking cigarettes or using alcohol and marijuana. A Weekly Reader survey of teens and preteens found that the number one reason given for using marijuana at all age levels was "to fit in with others."

Power

Remembering that the negative or discouraged approach to power is *rebellion,* it is easy to see how a rebellious teen can use drugs as a way of thumbing his nose at authority. "I can if I want to," he seems to be saying, "and there is nothing you can do to make me stop." The more demanding and authoritarian adults become, the more determined such a teen is to hold this destructive position.

For a teen low on self-esteem, drugs also offer a direct, if negative, means of attaining power.

For a teen low on self-esteem, drugs also offer a direct, if negative, means of attaining power. First, drugs themselves, as we have seen, are powerful substances. The teen who holds such power in his hand may experience the illusion that he too is powerful. Many drugs actually make the user feel powerful for a time (though ironically, the drugs eventually become addictive and thus take power over the user). There is also a social power involved with teens who themselves become dealers of drugs. Again, for a teen who is not getting her self-esteem from school, family or friends, becoming the source for drugs can make her suddenly become a very important person. Finally, there is economic power. Particularly among low-income teens, the big money available from selling drugs is a lure that many find irresistible.

Protection

The negative approach to protection is *revenge,* and drugs offer teens a harsh way of getting revenge against parents whom they feel have hurt them. Because our goal as parents is to see our teens survive and thrive, they can always hurt us by failing. Drugs are a way to fail "big time," and many parents have felt devastated as they watched their teenagers slowly self-destruct on alcohol and other drugs.

Withdrawal

A teen who lacks self-esteem may eventually give up trying to succeed through positive means, and instead *avoid* the challenges that life poses. Alcohol and other drugs, with their mind-altering, feel-good effects, are an easy way to do this. The teen who walks around in a blurry high no longer cares about the problems that he or she felt incapable of dealing with. As the old alcoholic slogan attests, they are finally "feeling no pain." (Of course, when the high wears off, the problems are not only still there, but compounded by the physiological effects of the drugs. This "crash," as it is often called, can be accompanied by physical pain, depression and even suicidal thinking.)

Challenge

The discouraged teen seeks an outlet for the goal of challenge through *thrill*

seeking. Excitement for excitement's sake, rather than a real testing and developing of one's mettle, becomes the fascination. Alcohol and other drugs become quick ways of getting a thrill. The mind-boggling effects of the drugs, as well as the inherent risks involved in using an illegal and potentially deadly substance, only heighten the excitement. Unfortunately for such teens, the only way to maintain the excitement level is to use more and more potent drugs, an escalating cycle usually ending in tragedy.

Stages of Drug Use

Drug use frequently progresses in four stages:

1. The experimentation phase

About 95% of all teens will try alcohol or marijuana. This is not to say that all of them suffer from low self-esteem and discouragement. The majority are motivated by simple curiosity. They have seen alcohol used by the adults in their life, and have watched alcohol and drugs used in TV and movies for years (often, unfortunately, in an overly glamorized way). They wonder, "What's it like?" Besides, "Everyone tries it."

2. The social use phase

About three-fourths of the teens who enter the experimentation phase move on

to stage two — social use. These teens will use alcohol and other drugs at parties and in other social settings, often mimicking adult behavior.

3. Seekers

In this third phase, the teen will actively seek out places where drugs can be found. It is usually in this phase that the addiction process begins.

4. Habitual use

Teens who move into the habitual use phase are no longer capable of making a free choice. The alcohol or other drug has become an addiction.

Drug use can be stopped at any stage.

Fortunately, although a teen can go through all four stages in just a few months, the progression is not inevitable. Drug use can be stopped at any stage. However, the more involved children and teens are with drugs, the more difficult it is for them to stop. The best way to fight drug use, therefore, is to prevent it. Educating children about the harmful effects of drugs long before the teen years is ideal. However, when that isn't possible, there is still a lot that we as parents can do.

Prevention: What You Can Do

In a very real sense, all of the Active Parenting skills that you have been learning in Chapters 1-8 are good drug prevention techniques. Because teens with low self-esteem and a lack of courage are the most likely to become seekers and habitual users, all of the encouragement influences discussed in Session II are essential. Because drug use is essentially a choice, helping your teen develop a sense of responsibility as presented in Session III will enable her to look clearly at the consequences of such use. Finally, the communication skills presented in Session IV will help you build a cooperative relationship with your teen, one in which you can talk together about these matters.

The following chart is designed to help you think about ways to use your Active Parenting skills to prevent alcohol and other drug use.

How to use your Active Parenting skills to prevent the use of alcohol and other drugs.

Active Parenting principle	Connection to drug use	What parents can do
BELONGING and CONTACT	Teens often use drugs to "fit in," thereby increasing their sense of belonging, and with it their self-esteem.	• Look for ways to increase the teen's sense of belonging to positive groups: the family, clubs, youth groups, teams and other extracurricular activity groups. • Encourage participation in the family through chores, participating in problem solving and decision making.
COURAGE and SELF-ESTEEM	Low self-esteem leads to discouragement which leads to negative behavior, including drug use.	• Provide teen with a steady diet of encouragement. • Avoid discouragement, especially perfectionism. • Provide opportunities for success; if teen has trouble in school, meet with counselors to determine what extra help is needed; find other areas for excellence through sports, hobbies or other outside interests. • Recognize the courage it takes for a teen to "just say no" to drugs; be supportive of teen to stand up to peer pressure.
RESPONSIBILITY	Teens who have learned personal responsibility will see the destructive consequences of drug use, and make better decisions.	• Teach responsibility by allowing choices and consequences. • Establish clear limits by setting and enforcing a "no use" rule. Help teen evaluate alternative ways of saying "no," and practice them. • Encourage participation in family decisions through family council meetings. • Allow expression of thoughts and feelings.
COOPERATION	Establishing a cooperative relationship will both reduce the rebellion and revenge motivation for drug use and help you become an "askable parent," one whom your teen will talk to about matters such as drug use and sexuality.	• Avoid communication blocks while using active communication skills. • Discuss drug use with your teen regularly. • Know the facts regarding drugs and their dangers. • Role play with your teen situations where they are pressured to use drugs.

Ten Parental Roles in the Prevention of Drug Use

The Office of Substance Abuse Prevention (OSAP) of the United States government recently formed an "Expert Panel" to advise parents on how they can help prevent the use of alcohol and other drugs in their children and teens. One of the outcomes of this panel, on which I was privileged to serve, was the description of 10 roles that parents can play in the prevention effort. Let's look at each:

1. The Parent as Role Model

One of the most powerful ways to teach our children is through our own example. As someone once said, values are caught, not taught. What we teach about the use of drugs and alcohol is as much a matter of our own use of substances as anything else. For example:

If you use illegal substances, your teen learns that the laws in this area don't matter; furthermore, since you are sneaking, he can sneak too.

If you get drunk, your teen learns that the use of alcohol does not need to be restrained.

If you drink, then drive, your teen learns to do the same.

One of the most powerful ways to teach our children is through our own example.

If you never seem to be having fun without a drink in your hand, your teen assumes that alcohol is the way to have fun.

...On the other hand:

If you follow the laws of the land and express your disapproval when a news item or TV show portrays others who don't, your teen learns that laws are to be obeyed.

If you choose to drink, and do so moderately, your teen will learn that when he is of legal age, he can drink moderately also.

If you carefully avoid drinking and driving, your teen will learn safety.

If you don't have to drink on every social occasion, your teen will learn that alcohol isn't a necessity for a good time.

And if you do what you say you value, your teen will learn to respect you as a person of integrity.

2. The Parent as Educator

The information that your teen has picked up on the street or in the schoolyard about alcohol and other drugs is likely to be one-sided. Teens often learn about the exciting effects of drugs, how much fun getting high and partying can be, even how to use drug paraphernalia and where to "score" (buy) drugs. What they don't get told clearly is how dangerous and destructive drugs are.

To remedy this information bias, many schools have instituted drug-related programs to help inform children and teens about the real dangers involved in substance use. If you are fortunate to have such a program in your school system, find out exactly what the program is teaching. Besides making sure the program fits with your own value system, you will probably also learn more about drug use and abuse — information you can share with your teen.

In any event, you will also want to sit down with your teen (and preteens if you have any) and discuss this thoroughly. Some things to keep in mind before you have this talk:

To be convincing, you need more than emotion, you need facts.

■ Be prepared. To be convincing, you need more than emotion, you need facts. Know why each drug is harmful, especially nicotine, alcohol and marijuana, as many teens mistakenly think these are harmless. In addition to the chart at the end of this chapter, you can get pamphlets from your teen's school or from the government's Office of Health.

■ Don't get hooked into an argument. Your teen may resist the facts now, but consider them more later...unless you've become overbearing and disrespectful, thus giving him a reason to rebel.

■ Keep the tone friendly and invite your teen's input.

■ This isn't a one-shot deal. Have similar discussions from time to time, bringing in magazine articles and other new information. Ask your teen to collect information too.

The Genetic Connection

Although it is beyond the scope of this program to present all of the information that you will want to know about alcohol and other drugs, there is one item that is important to consider. There is increasing evidence that alcoholism, and perhaps other drug addictions, have a strong genetic component. In other words, the tendency to become addicted is passed from generation to generation.

What this means is that some people do not have the physical makeup to handle alcohol, and ought not to drink *at all.* If alcoholism has occurred in your family, there is a high risk that your teens may also have a physical constitution that cannot tolerate alcohol. In such families it is a good idea for the parent to explain these facts to the teen, and to begin teaching the teen that "in our family we stay away from alcohol, as well as illegal drugs, altogether."

3. Making and Enforcing a "No Use" Rule

One of the themes of Active Parenting has been the importance of allowing teens freedom within limits. This is consistent with life in our democratic society, and our goal of preparing them to survive and thrive in this society. The limits to freedom in our society are called laws. In the family these limits are called "rules." Should a teen break these rules, then he or she must experience a natural or logical consequence, because it is this combination of choice plus consequence that teaches responsibility.

Certain drugs are illegal for everyone, while others can be used only by adults.

Unless we are morally opposed to a law (in which case we can choose to exercise our right of civil disobedience and go to jail), it is our responsibility to obey the law and teach our children to do the same. The laws regarding the use of alcohol and other drugs are very specific. Certain drugs are illegal for everyone, while others can be used only by adults. It is important for you to support these laws by establishing a clear and consistent "no use" rule in your family. The rule can be stated like this:

> **"No use of illegal drugs by anyone in the family, and no use of alcohol or nicotine by anyone under the legal age of ___."**

The no use rule can be part of your discussion about the effects of alcohol and other drugs, and all members of the family who are old enough to understand it can sign it.

Once the rule is established, it is important for you to let your teen know that you expect him or her to abide by the rule.

Once the rule is established, it is important for you to let your teen know that you expect him or her to abide by the rule. This means no experimenting or social use either. We don't want to sabotage our own rule by giving the message that "all kids will try it" or that "rules were made to be broken."

If you do want your teen to satisfy his or her curiosity about what alcohol or tobacco is like, it may be legal for you to allow the use of these substances in your own home. However, in some states it is illegal even under these controlled conditions, so be sure to check the laws in your state first. If you choose to provide this safe opportunity to try them, we strongly recommend that you make this a one time event, and DO NOT ALLOW REGULAR USE. It is clear that tobacco is a major health hazard at any age, and there is growing evidence that alcohol can interfere with normal teenage development. Of course, marijuana and other illegal substances should not be used by anyone.

For rules to carry impact, they must be backed up by consequences.

For rules to carry impact, they must be backed up by consequences. The use of logical consequences as described in Chapter 6 is recommended to help enforce the no use rule. If you have no reason to suspect drug use, then we suggest you discuss consequences in general terms. You might say something like:

"Let's be clear about something. For us to continue to feel good about giving you more freedom and more responsibility, we have to be able to trust you. This no use rule is largely a matter of trust. We won't be there looking over your shoulder every minute, nor do we feel the need to keep you locked in your room during all your free time. But if you should break that trust, then the responsible thing for us to do as your parents is to keep a closer eye on you. That means keeping you home more often, checking up on you more regularly, and otherwise cutting down on your freedom. And since using alcohol or other drugs when driving can be deadly, we'd want to protect you and others from your using the car."

If your teen has a history of drug or alcohol use, or breaks the no use rule, then the consequences can get more specific. Rather than rely on the common and usually ineffectual consequence of grounding, it is better to use privileges, possessions and favors that the teen wants from you. Remember, it is important that these consequences be logically related to the broken no use rule. The loss of the car, which was mentioned earlier, is logically connected to the use of mind-altering substances because of the safety factor. Not being allowed to go to parties or concerts for a period of time is logical in that these are trust situ-

ations, and your teen has temporarily lost your trust. By talking with your teen, your spouse and other adults, you can come up with a list of consequences that will be meaningful to the teen.

Keep in mind also that it is important for you to specify how your teen can earn back your trust. If he feels that he can never win back your trust, or that his freedom is gone forever, he may decide to openly rebel, and do what he wants to do anyway.

4. Parents as Stimulators of Healthy Activity

We have discussed how the individual's desire for challenge peaks during the teen years. When a healthy outlet for this normal goal cannot be found, teenagers are prone to turn to the discouraged approach of excitement seeking. Activities such as stealing, vandalism, practicing promiscuous sexuality, drinking alcohol and taking drugs all offer easy thrills for the discouraged excitement seeker.

Cycling, rock climbing, white-water canoeing and kayaking add an element of natural challenge that has a host of positive effects.

In many ways life has become so comfortable in our society that there are not many natural challenges for teenagers to face. We no longer have to pit ourselves against the elements to survive, and we have managed to create an economy that does not require the participation of our youth in any meaningful way. Still, there are ways for creative parents to encourage healthy activity in our children.

Sports offer excellent opportunities to meet the challenge goal in positive ways. Organized team sports, from basketball to swimming, are still viable, and youth leagues such as the YMCA offer a chance for every teen to participate. Other sports such as cycling, rock climbing, white-water canoeing and kayaking add an element of natural challenge that has a host of positive effects. In fact, camping and other wilderness programs have proven to be so healthy that many successful treatment programs for teens are built around these activities. As preventive activities, scouting and other outdoor organizations are still excellent.

5. Parents as Consultants and Educators on Peer Pressure

Most people realize that to "just say no" is a lot easier said than done. When

was the last time that you knuckled under to peer pressure and ate something off your diet, or bought something you didn't really want? The pressures on teens and preteens, with their heightened desire to belong, are a whole lot stronger.

Parents can play an important role in supporting teens in their efforts to stand up to negative peer pressure. Since peer pressure resistance takes a lot of courage, all of the encouragement techniques described in Session II are extremely important. In addition it is important for

It is important for your child to learn the skills needed to resist peer pressure.

your child to learn the skills needed to resist peer pressure. These "resistance skills," as they are often called, are now taught in many high schools, junior highs and middle schools. If your teen's school does teach such a program, you can become involved by helping your teen practice these skills at home.

In any case you can talk with your teens about ways of resisting peer pressure. What can they say or do that will avoid the drug invitation, and yet minimize the risk that they will be totally ostracized by the group? One approach we call "How to say 'no' and not look like a jerk," suggests five steps* that you can teach, and practice with, your teens. Let's look at an example:

Step 1. Ask questions.

Troublemaker:	"Let's go over to my house after school."
Skill user:	"What are we going to do?"
Troublemaker:	"Well, my folks are away."
Skill user:	"So?"
Troublemaker:	"I thought we'd try a couple of beers."

*Copyright 1986 Roberts Fitzmahan & Associates, Inc., Seattle, Washington, all rights reserved. Used by permission of Comprehensive Health Education Foundation, Seattle, Washington.

Asking questions gives the skill user the information he or she needs to avoid trouble. Children can stop asking questions as soon as they know they are being asked to do something that could get them into trouble.

Step 2. Name the trouble.

Skill user: "That's illegal; that's 'minor in possession.' Besides, it's against my family's rules."

Naming the trouble identifies the problem with the suggested activity from the skill user's point of view.

Step 3. Identify the consequences.

Skill user: "If I did that, I could be arrested. My parents would place me on restriction. Then I wouldn't be able to have any friends over, watch television or even talk on the phone."

Naming the consequences provides the skill user's reason for staying out of trouble.

Step 4. Suggest an alternative.

Skill user: "Why don't we go down to the basketball court and shoot some baskets instead?"

By suggesting an alternative, the skill user communicates to his friend that he is saying no to trouble but not to the friendship. He also presents a different, more positive way to have fun together that avoids trouble.

Step 5. Walk and talk and leave the door open.

Troublemaker: "No, I don't think so. That sounds pretty boring to me."

Skill user (moving away from his friend): "If you change your mind, I'll be at the court until 5:30. I'll bet you an ice cream that you can't beat me one-on-one."

Even if the friend doesn't accept the alternative, the skill user stays in control by leaving the situation, and saves face by leaving the door open to his friend to join him in a positive activity.

6. Parents as Monitors and Supervisors

I heard a tragic story the other day. A fight broke out at a party between teens from two rival high schools. There had been a lot of beer drinking, and everyone was feeling pretty macho. During the fight one of the teens pulled a knife and stabbed another, who died on the way to the hospital. This tragedy was not West Side Story. It took place in an affluent suburb of a typical American city.

It is part of our job as parents to get in the way.

You may expect that the parents of the house were out of town, as is often the case with teen parties. They were not. In fact, they were upstairs watching TV. When asked why they were not downstairs supervising the party, they answered, "Because we didn't want to get in the way."

Their response is not that unusual. The irony, however, is that it is part of our job as parents to get in the way. We must be willing and able to continue to provide safe limits to our children's freedom until they become capable of doing it on their own. Nowhere is this concept of freedom within expanding limits more important than where alcohol and other drugs are involved. The research clearly shows that good parental supervision is a key factor in preventing delinquency, drug use and school failure. Although it is unwise to try to monitor every moment of the teen's day, teens who have a great deal of unsupervised time are at a much higher risk for drifting into problem peer groups, and then developing problems themselves.

It is important for parents to be awake when the teen comes home.

The key for parents is to know where our children and teens are and with whom. As they demonstrate responsibility in handling unstructured time, we can gradually relax our supervision. Even in families where both parents work outside the home, telephone check-ins after school or supervised activities that the teen participates in can help parents monitor behavior. In addition to knowing where the teen is going in the evening and with whom, it is important to have agreed-upon curfews, and for the parents to be awake when the teen comes home. Sitting down with your teen and cooperatively setting house rules for these matters is a good way to reduce later conflicts and misunderstandings. If the teen does a good job of keeping to the agreed-upon limits, her responsibility should earn her greater freedom. Likewise, if the rules are broken, then logical consequences can be used to reduce freedom.

7. Parents Working with Other Parents

Teens have tremendous support groups to back up their behavior. Unfortunately, this support is often negative, and the behavior often involves alcohol and other drugs. The principle, however, is accurate: There is power in numbers. Parents can also utilize this principle by forming parent support groups in the community. These "parent networks," as they are often called, can help parents agree on certain issues such as chaperoning, curfews, the need for regular communication among parents, and the unacceptability of alcohol and other drugs being used by children and teens.

If your teen's school does not already have a parents' network, you can use this Active Parenting group to begin one.

The strength of developing community guidelines for such issues is reflected in a quote by the great French general Napoleon. He observed that "People do not want liberty; they want equality." This is particularly true of teens. Parents know the feeling of an uphill battle when they hear the age-old retort, "But everyone else is...." How much easier it is for the teen to give up something he wants when none of the other teens are being allowed to do it either.
If your teen's school does not already have a parents' network, you can use this Active Parenting group to begin one. Just talk to your group leader about how you can continue to meet, and expand your efforts from there.

8. Parents as Identifiers and Confronters of Drug Use

We talked earlier about the importance of establishing a no use rule in your family. However, for any rule to be effective, the parent must be willing to expend the energy to detect when the rule has been violated. One of the best ways to determine whether children or teens have broken the rule is to notice their behavior when they come in at night. Do they act incoherent or suspicious? Do you smell alcohol on their breath? Are their pupils dilated? Three signs almost always mean that your child is becoming involved in drug use:

Notice your teen's behavior when they come in at night.

1) possession of drug-related paraphernalia such as pipes, rolling papers, small decongestant bottles or small butane lighters;

2) possession of drugs themselves or evidence of drugs (peculiar plants, butts, seeds or leaves in ashtrays or clothing pockets); and

3) the odor of alcohol or other drugs or the smell of incense or other cover-up scents.

There are other signs that are not conclusive in themselves, but a combination of several of these usually means that your child is not only around alcohol or other drugs but is actually using them:

- Heavy identification with the drug culture (drug-related magazines, slogans on clothing, conversations and jokes that are preoccupied with drugs, and hostility when discussing drugs).

- Signs of physical deterioration (memory lapses, short attention span, difficulty in concentration, poor physical coordination, slurred or incoherent speech, unhealthy appearance, indifference to hygiene and grooming, bloodshot eyes, dilated pupils). Again, these things are often harmless characteristics of the teenage years, but when many of these appear together, it's time to suspect alcohol or other drug use.

- Dramatic changes in school performance. A distinct downward turn in your child's grades (not just from Cs to Fs, but from As to Bs to Cs), more and more uncompleted assignments and increased absenteeism or tardiness.

- Changes in behavior such as chronic dishonesty (lying, stealing and cheating); trouble with the police; changes in friends; evasiveness in talking about new friends; possession of large amounts of money; increasing and inappropriate anger, hostility, irritability and secretiveness; reduced motivation, energy, self-discipline and self-esteem; and a diminished interest in extracurricular activities and hobbies.

Although all of these symptoms have been found to be associated with alcohol and other drug use, you should not draw conclusions on the basis of one or two of these symptoms. Look for an overall pattern of behavior.

In any discussion of detection, parents always ask whether they should search a child's room. We should show our children and teenagers the same respect that the law, in general, shows us. A police officer may not come into your home and go through your belongings without probable cause and a search warrant; similarly, we ought not to make a routine habit of searching our children's belongings. However, if you have reasonable grounds to believe that a child is harmfully involved with alcohol or other drugs, I do believe you have the right to go through the child's belongings in search of hard evidence with which to confront the child.

One reason that I believe this is justified is that it's almost impossible to find out whether a teenager is involved in alcohol or other drugs by asking him or her.

By becoming involved, the teenager makes a decision to lie.

Confronting a child or teenager.

The earlier a drug problem is found and faced, the less difficult it is to overcome.

Parents frequently deny the evidence and postpone confronting their children. The earlier a drug problem is found and faced, the less difficult it is to overcome. If you suspect your child of using alcohol or other drugs, you must first deal with your anger, resentment and guilt.

Do not take your child's alcohol or other drug use as a sign that you are a bad parent. Remember that parenting is not the only influence on a child's development.

If you are married, make an agreement with your partner about how to handle the situation. It is essential that you present a unified front, as any disagreement between the two of you will be exploited by your child.

Do not try to have a confrontation while your teen is under the influence of the drug. If your teen is unconscious or semi-conscious, take him or her immediately to a detoxification center or a hospital emergency room. Do not make the mistake of allowing your child to "sleep it off." In addition to the medical importance of seeking treatment, it also sends the clear message that drug use is serious business and is not going to be taken lightly.

Do not take your child's alcohol or other drug use as a sign that you are a bad parent.

Be careful not to react with rage or excessive anger. Although you may feel justified in becoming angry, a calm, firm reaction produces the best results. Trying to embarrass or humiliate your child is also likely to be counterproductive. Bribery does not work, either. The child will take the rewards, but continue to use alcohol or other drugs. Threats and unreasonable discipline also tend to drive the child further into alcohol or other drug use.

The discipline that works best is the imposition of logical consequences. This is the same discipline skill that is recommended for other violations of rules and limits. The key is to be firm, calm and caring. When we confront out of caring ("I'm doing this because I care about *you*") rather than rage ("I'm doing this because you're *bad*"), it is much more likely that our teens will respond positively.

Sit down with your partner, or if you are single, by yourself or with someone you trust, and plan how you will confront your child. (A single parent may want to ask an adult friend or relative to assist in the actual confrontation. There *is*

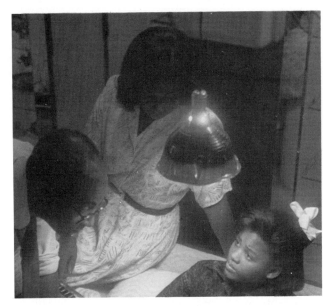

often strength in numbers.) Think of the evidence you have found and decide how to present the information in a respectful, yet forceful, manner. It is important that you back up each accusation with examples and evidence.

Think about your goals for the confrontation. If your child is already in the addicted or heavy use stage, your goal will be to get him or her into a treatment program. Consult your local mental health center, a physician, or a hospital that specializes in alcohol and other drug treatment. If your child is in one of the earlier stages of alcohol or other drug use, he or she still has a choice in the matter. Your goal might be to obtain an agreement to cease all drug use.

The discipline that works best is the imposition of logical consequences.

Be prepared for the child to try to divert you from the issue of his or her drug use. Children also tend to lie or make excuses or threats when confronted. They may threaten to run away, to behave even more inappropriately, or even to commit suicide. Take any threats seriously, but do not allow yourself to be blackmailed. It is particularly important to treat a suicide threat seriously. More and more teenagers are committing suicide. Contact a crisis center, suicide hotline or mental health center immediately. They can help you assess the situation and determine if the suicide threat is serious or just manipulative. Do not try to make this determination yourself.

Another guideline to keep in mind during the confrontation is to act more and talk less. Our lectures almost always fall on deaf ears when a child is already involved in alcohol or other drugs. The logical consequences that you devise and enforce will capture your child's attention.

9. Parents as Managers of Intoxicated Children

We have already stressed the importance of attaining immediate medical help for a teen who has consumed a large amount of alcohol and is unconscious or semi-conscious. Because teens often combine alcohol with other drugs, the danger is multiplied and should always be treated seriously. When in doubt, the best rule of thumb is to call the emergency room of a nearby hospital.

Whenever an alcohol or other drug-related problem exists, the parents should consider seeking professional help. With stage one or two use, the parents' own confrontation and intervention may be sufficient. However, by stage three, and certainly if addiction (stage four) has occurred, then contacting a drug treatment program or outpatient drug and alcohol specialist is called for. Your Active Parenting group leader or your family physician can help you decide whom to call.

10. Parents as Managers of Their Own Feelings

As serious as a drug problem is to a family, reacting with panic, anger and hysteria only makes it worse. If you find that your anger needs venting, take a walk, yell and scream in a closed room, beat a pillow, or call a friend to talk it out. In other words, exit; don't explode. You want to be able to confront the problem, and your teen, in a calm yet firm manner. Anger will usually just provoke a power struggle and escalate the problem.

Confront the problem, and your teen, in a calm yet firm manner.

Be aware of the tendency for well-meaning parents to feel guilty when faced with such a situation. You may have made mistakes in your parenting (we all have), but it is the teen who is responsible for the choice to use or not use drugs. Allowing yourself to be hooked into feeling guilty will make it difficult for you to present a firm stance on the issue.

Finally, keep in mind that in this, as in all of parenting, we are dealing with influence rather than control. You may do everything in this program and more to influence your children and teens not to use alcohol and other drugs. And yet they may still get influenced by others to do so. We can only do what we can do. Fortunately, by using the principles and skills presented in this program, we can improve the odds that our teens will make healthy choices.

Family Enrichment Activity #5

Teaching Skills

Part of developing a positive sense of self-esteem is seeing oneself as a capable individual. When we take the time to teach our teens skills, we not only help them become more capable, but also give them positive ways of achieving the goals of power and challenge. In fact, teaching your teen a skill empowers her in a very positive way, and enriches your relationship with her.

The following steps can help you teach a skill effectively:

1. Motivate: Encourage your teen to want to learn the skill by explaining the value the skill has to the teen or the entire family.

For example: "We learned a great way of saying 'no' to alcohol and other drugs that doesn't make you look like a jerk. I think you'll really like it."

2. Select a good time: Pick a time when neither you nor your teen will feel rushed or upset by other things.

3. Demonstrate: Show your teen how to perform the skill, explaining slowly as you do.

For example: "The first step is to ask questions. Watch as your mother role plays a friend trying to get me to go drink beer at her house while her parents are out."

4. Let your teen try: Let your teen perform the skill while you stand by ready to offer help if he needs it. Be gentle about mistakes, and let it be fun.

For example: "Okay, now why don't I play the troublemaker, and you use the five steps to saying 'no' without looking like a jerk."

5. Work together: Once your teen has learned the skill, you can sometimes work along together, so that you can both enjoy the companionship of the activity.

6. Acknowledge the efforts: Make comments about your teen's efforts and progress.

For example: "You're really getting the hang of this. That was a great alternative that you came up with this time."

"Teaching Skills"

Remember When...

Recall a skill that one of your parents taught you. Again, close your eyes for a moment and visualize the learning experience.

What was the activity?

_____

How did you feel about your parent at that moment?

_____

How did you feel about yourself?

_____

What can you learn from the memory:

Mistakes to avoid:

_____

Actions to do:

_____

Now You Try!

Pick an activity you would like to work on with your teen this week. Possible activities are:

- A sport skill
- Something to do with the car
- Cooking a special dish
- Something to do with your job
- How to open a checking or savings account
- But we especially recommend the "How to say 'no' and not look like a jerk" skill presented on pages 148 and 149.

Talk it over with your teens, and list skills you will teach.

	TEEN'S NAME	SKILL TO BE TAUGHT
1.	_____	_____
2.	_____	_____
3.	_____	_____

"Teaching Skills"

After you teach the skill, use the six steps as a checklist:

1. Did you MOTIVATE the child?

2. Did you SELECT A GOOD TIME when you weren't rushed?

3. Did you DEMONSTRATE the skill?

4. Did you LET HIM OR HER TRY?

5. Did you WORK ALONGSIDE your teen?

6. Did you ACKNOWLEDGE HIS OR HER EFFORTS?

What went well with each teen?

1. _____

2. _____

3. _____

What might you do to improve the experience next time?

_____

_____

_____

If you chose to teach your teens "HOW TO SAY 'NO' WITHOUT LOOKING LIKE A JERK," did you teach each step?

Step 1. Ask questions.

Step 2. Name the trouble.

Step 3. Identify the consequences.

Step 4. Suggest an alternative.

Step 5. Walk and talk and leave the door open.

The Parent as Role Model

Think about the example you set for your teen through your own use of alcohol or other drugs. Is it consistent with what you want your teen to learn about adult use?

1. How do I use alcohol and other drugs?

_____

2. What is this modeling to my teen?

_____

3. What do I want to change, if anything, to be a better model?

_____

The "No Use" Discussion

In preparing for your discussion, think about key information and points you want to cover. List them here:

_____

_____

Prepare an agreement on a full sheet of paper that all of you can sign. The agreement might say something like: "We agree that for the health and safety of our family, no one in the family will use illegal drugs, and there will be no use of alcohol or nicotine by minors."

After your "no use" discussion, think about how it went:

What went well about your talk?_____

What problems came up that you might like some help in handling?_____

Did you get everyone to sign the agreement?_____

If not, what can you do differently next time to get agreement?_____

Drug Reference Chart

	TRADE OR OTHER NAMES	POSSIBLE EFFECTS	EFFECTS OF OVERDOSE	WITHDRAWAL SYNDROME
NARCOTICS				
Opium	Dover's Powder, Paregoric, Parepectolin	Euphoria, drowsiness, respiratory depression, constricted pupils, nausea	Slow and shallow breathing, clammy skin, convulsions, coma, possible death	Watery eyes, runny nose, yawning, loss of appetite, irritability, tremors, panic, chills and sweating, cramps, nausea
Morphine	Morphine, Pectoral Syrup			
Codeine	Tylenol with Codeine, Empirin Compound with Codeine, Robitussin A-C			
Heroin				
Meperidine (Pethidine)				
Methadone				
Other Narcotics				
DEPRESSANTS				
*Chloral Hydrate	Noctec, Somnos	Slurred speech, disorientation, drunken behavior *No odor	Shallow respiration, clammy skin, dilated pupils, weak and rapid pulse, coma, possible death	Anxiety, insomnia, tremors, delirium, convulsions, possible death
*Barbiturates	Phenobarbital, Tuinal, Amytal, Nembutal, Seconal, Lotusate			
*Benzodiazepines	Ativan, Azene, Clanopin, Dalmane, Diazepam, Librium, Xanex, Serax, Tranxene, Valium, Verstran, Halcion, Paxipam, Restoril			
*Methaquatone	Quaalude			
Alcohol				

Chapter 10 - Ten Parental Roles in the Prevention of Drug Use

	TRADE OR OTHER NAMES	POSSIBLE EFFECTS	EFFECTS OF OVERDOSE	WITHDRAWAL SYNDROME
STIMULANTS				
Cocaine	Coke, Flake, Snow	Increased alertness, excitation, euphoria, increased pulse rate and blood pressure, insomnia, loss of appetite	Agitation, increase in body temperature hallucinations, convulsions, possible death	Apathy, long periods of sleep, irritability, depression, disorientation
Amphetamines	Biphetamine, Delcobese, Desoxyn, Dexedrine Mediatric			
HALLUCINOGENS				
LSD	Acid, Microdot	Illusions and hallucinations, poor perception of time and distance	Longer, more intense "trip"epi-sodes, psychosis, possible death	Withdrawal syndrome not reported
Mescaline and Peyote	Mesc, Buttons, Cactus			
Amphetamine Variants	2,5-DMA,PMA, STP, MDA, MDMA, TMA, DOM, DOB			
Phencyclidine	PCP, Angel Dust, Hog			
Phencyclidine Analogs	**PCE, PCYy, TCP**			
Other Hallucinogens	Bufotenine, Ibogaine, DMT, DET, psilocybin, Psilocyn			
CANNABIS				
Marijuana	Pot, Acapulco Gold, Grass, Reefer, Sinsemilla, Thai Sticks	Euphoria, relaxed inhibitions, increased appetite, disoriented behavior	Fatigue, paranoia, possible psychosis	Insomnia, hyperactivity, and decreased appetite occasionally reported
Tetrahydro-cannabinol	THC			
Hashish	Hash			

Parenting
and Teen
Sexuality

Chapter 11

Understanding Teen Sexuality

A group of teenage girls huddle together around a table at lunchtime in the high school cafeteria. Their attention is at 100 percent as they take turns swapping stories about their sexual adventures, using graphic language that would burn the ears of today's hottest romance writers. They are laughing enthusiastically as one of the girls recounts how she and her boyfriend got stoned last weekend, then left the party early to "do it" in the back seat of her parents' car while it was still parked in the garage.

As she gives the specifics of how he did what to her and where, and how each touch felt, she notices that one of the girls isn't laughing. "What's the matter?" the storyteller asks, "Don't you know what we're talking about?"

"No, I don't," responds the quiet girl. "I've never done that."

"You're still a virgin?!" another girl asks tauntingly. She nods affirmatively. And in the brief but pointed conversation that follows, the quiet girl picks up a nickname. From now until she either graduates or succumbs to the peer pressure, she will be known as "Snow White, the Goody-Goody Little Virgin."

Facts about Teen Sexuality

If this scenario sounds quite different from one that might have occurred in your own school days, consider the following:

- 57% of 12- to 17-year-olds have had sexual intercourse.

- Only 43% have talked with their parents about sex.

In addition to the value questions raised by these statistics, there is the more obvious concern about pregnancy and disease:

- Four in every 10 teenage girls become pregnant before they are 20 years old.

- Teen pregnancy rates in the U.S. are among the highest in any industrialized nation.

- Fewer than 20% of teens use contraception the first few times they have sex.

- 40% of teen pregnancies result in abortion.

- Pregnant teens have a high risk of toxemia, anemia and death.

- Pregnancy is a major reason for suicide among teens.

- The psychological trauma of bearing a child, having one's child adopted or having an abortion is great.

- Children born to teen mothers have a high risk of prematurity, low birth weight and retardation.

- Only 50% of teenage girls who give birth before age 18 ever complete high school (compared with 96% of females who wait until after age 20).

- Only 70% of teen fathers complete high school.

- Teen mothers earn about half as much income as those who give birth in their 20s; most of their babies end up on welfare roles.

- 40% of the girls who run away from home each year do so because they are pregnant.

- The rate of sexually transmitted disease among 16- to 20-year-olds is three times that of the general population.

- Sexually active teens risk infection with the AIDS virus which is fatal.

What This Chapter Is
and Is *Not* about

Most parents agree that it would be better for teenagers to postpone sexual intercourse, at least until they become adults.

The statistics concerning teenage sexuality are enough to make any reasonable parent worry. The problems that have always been associated with teenage pregnancy are still with us, and now, with the advent of AIDS, suddenly sex has become even more dangerous. In addition, the fragile identities of most teen-agers make them particularly vulnerable to sexual exploitation and otherwise going too far too fast. Most parents agree that it would be better for teenagers to postpone sexual intercourse (as well as other heavy sexual conduct) at least until they become adults.

Your own values, as well as your religious orientation, will help you determine what you will communicate to your children.

This session is designed to help you apply Active Parenting principles towards helping your teen develop into a healthy sexual adult. Because our common goal is so important, it is critical that we not become sidetracked by debating the controversial issues of our times: abortion, homosexuality and birth control. Your own values, as well as your religious orientation, will help you determine *what* you will communicate to your children about these issues. We will help you determine *how*. Of course, what our children ultimately come to value will be their choice, because in the area of sexuality, as in all areas of parenting, we can only *influence* their decisions; the *control* is in their hands.

Teens and Sexuality

The pressures on teens, described in Session V, to become involved with drugs and alcohol are doubled when it comes to becoming sexually active. The reason is straightforward. Most of the pressure to try drugs for the first time comes from the outside, from peers. With sexuality, however, not only is there outside peer pressure, but somewhere between ages 11 and 13 the teen hits puberty, and hormonal pressures come into play from the inside. For most of history the onset of puberty (and the accompanying sexual desires) and the age when teens married have been very close together. For example, the most famous lovers of all time, Romeo and Juliet, were only about 14 years old. However, the onset of puberty is occurring at a younger age today, while people are waiting longer to marry. Therefore, teens are expected to deny these pressures longer than ever before. Couple these factors with the focus on sexuality in our society (from commercials, movies and music to the way we dress and act), and it is little wonder that so many of our teenagers are giving in to the pressure to become sexually active.

Tasks of Adolescence

Two of the most important tasks that any teenager faces are to accept oneself as a sexual being and to develop a philosophy of life. Let's look at each:

1. To accept one self as a sexual being.

As a person matures from a child to an adult, the changes which occur in sexual development are of great concern. Pubescent boys will sit around comparing penis size and amounts of pubic hair (or at least steal comparative glimpses in the locker room), while girls almost always are concerned about the size of their

breasts or when they will start to menstruate. If our society as a whole exaggerates the importance of sexuality, and physical beauty, teens do so tenfold. With so many teenagers overemphasizing slimness (to the extreme of developing eating disorders such as anorexia or bulimia), helping our teenagers become comfortable with *their* bodies, whatever the size and shape, requires sensitivity and understanding. It also requires a recognition on our part that in sexuality, as in all areas, it's not what you have that's important; it's what you do with what you have.

Part of accepting oneself as a sexual being is accepting the sexual feelings that come with puberty. There is nothing dirty or

Helping our teenagers become comfortable with their bodies, whatever the size and shape, requires sensitivity and understanding.

wrong about wanting to make passionate love with the sex object across the room in geometry. Nature has given us a sex drive so that we will continue the species, and it is natural to want to "do it." The challenge of parenting, however, is to help our teens recognize that human beings are capable of a higher, more fulfilling level of sex than the just "doing it" sex of other animals. In other words, we can accept that we have an animal nature and not feel ashamed of this, but strive to restrain this part of our behavior in favor of our more human capabilities. We can learn to postpone sexual behavior until we are older, and in circumstances consistent with our beliefs and values. This leads to the second task of adolescence:

2. To develop a philosophy of life on which to base decisions.

Teenagers are, by and large, philosophers. They have a view on everything and an opinion about everyone. This is part of their process of developing a sense of values, and an overall philosophy of life from which to operate. The sexuality aspect of this philosophy involves questions about how the teen values men and

By using effective communication skills, we can help our teens develop a philosophy of life on which to base decisions.

women; what responsibility the teen has for his or her sexual partner; whether the teen will choose to delay gratification or act out immediate desires; and how sex and love will be integrated or separated. By using effective communication skills, we can help our teens find positive answers to these and other questions.

Sexuality and the Five Goals of Teen Behavior

When self-esteem is high, and the teen feels courageous, he is more able to pursue his sexual development through the positive approaches.

Sex can be for better or for worse. It can be used as a means of achieving the five basic goals through either the positive or the negative approaches. The key, as with most behavior, lies in the Think-Feel-Do cycle. When self-esteem is high, and the teen feels courageous, he is more able to pursue his sexual development through the positive approaches. But when self-esteem is low, and a lack of courage results, it is easy to take the negative approaches along the path of immediate pleasure. Let's look more closely at both approaches to the five basic goals as they relate to sexuality:

Goal #1: Sexuality as a Path to Contact

Positive Approach: Responsible, Cooperative, Courageous Sexuality

Sexual contact offers human beings a powerful way to express their deepest feelings of belonging. When two people feel truly connected at an emotional level, to also connect on a physical level is one of the most exquisite experiences in the human condition. Unfortunately, many people have been taught to emphasize only one aspect of their sexuality, either the emotional or the physical. In our culture, boys are often taught to value the physical side of sex, while girls, the emotional side. Although this tendency is certainly changing, we want to continue to help our teens appreciate that full sexual contact means a combination of emotional and physical pleasure.

Negative Approach: Undue Attention Seeking

For a discouraged teen lacking self-esteem, sex offers an easy way to become the center of attention. The stories of boys in the locker room bragging about their sexual exploits is familiar to anyone who ever went to high school. Of course, with today's girls often becoming as adventurous as their male counterparts, this past time is no longer limited to boys.

For a discouraged teen lacking self-esteem, sex offers an easy way to become the center of attention.

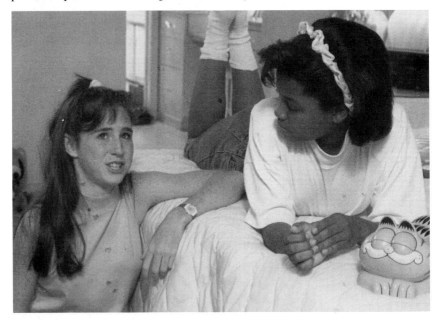

In addition, when a teenage girl lacks self-esteem and has doubts about herself, she may use sex as a way to be liked. In one survey, 70% of teen boys said they would lie to a girl by saying "I love you" in order to have sex. Girls with low self-esteem are vulnerable to this type of line, and may use sex as a way of getting undue attention and contact.

Goal #2: Sexuality as a Path to Power

Positive Approach: Independence from Peer Pressure

The idea that sex can be powerful is not new. As far back as the biblical stories of Samson and Delilah, sex has been one way that people sometimes exerted power over each other. In today's world of teenage sexuality, teens sometimes like to see how far they can get their partners to go, not for sexual reasons but to see how powerful they can be. "I got her into bed" can be a way to bolster a sagging self-esteem through a mistaken approach to power. Teens with the courage to achieve power in positive ways will not exploit their peers sexually. In fact, they can use their power to speak out against sexual disrespect and abuse. Parents can talk to their teens about these issues, and teach them how to use their power positively to say "no" to sexual advances. We can also teach them to recognize the sorts of lines frequently used by power hungry peers attempting to get them to give in. We can help them practice assertive responses so that they will be more powerful at resisting peer pressure.

Parents can teach their teens how to use their power positively, to say "no" to sexual advances.

We can also talk to them about having the power to resist the sexual urges that they feel within themselves. Most teens, at one time or another, will want to express their sexuality fully. It takes courage to postpone these internal desires, and a supportive parent who understands this and doesn't blame or judge can help.

Negative Approach: Rebellion

In addition to achieving power over one's peers through sexual acting out, discouraged teens often use sexual activity as a way to rebel against autocratic parents. The harder such parents come down on the teen's behavior, the more the teen is out to show the parent that "You can't control my body! I'll do as I like!" Rebellious teens often act as "reverse puppets." In other words, if you try to control them by pulling the string to the right hand, the left hand goes up. In order to feel powerful, they think they must do the opposite of what the parent orders. In effect, both the puppet AND the reverse puppet are controlled by the parent, since neither is free to choose his or her own course of action. With such teens, it is a mistake to use anger and punishment in an attempt to coerce them into the sexual behavior we want for them. It is better to back off, and approach them with palms up as a consultant.

It is a mistake to use anger and punishment, in an attempt to coerce teens into the sexual behavior we want for them.

Goal #3: Sexuality as a Path to Protection

Positive Approach: Assertiveness

We have already talked about how teens can use power and assertiveness skills to resist the undue pressures of their peers. In a larger sense, such teens learn to protect themselves directly by standing up to problems head-on. They are able to argue their point of view, even with parents, while struggling to develop a philosophy of life that includes a code of sexual conduct.

Negative Approach: Revenge

Whenever teens perceive that we have hurt them, either verbally or physically, they may attempt to even the score by hurting us back. One way to do this is to violate our value system, and sexual activity offers them an easy way to do this. In fact, if they really want to use sex to get even for real or perceived injustices, they can always become pregnant or get someone pregnant.

Goal #4: Sexuality as a Path to Withdrawal

Positive Approach: Centering

In Session I we discussed how everyone needs time to withdraw from the stresses of everyday life, to be alone and to center himself emotionally. Though adult sexuality is usually thought of as a special form of contact between two people, it also offers a welcome withdrawal from outside pressures. We have asked teenagers to resist this positive aspect of their lives until they are older, and can better cope with all the implications of sexual intercourse.

This leads to the question of masturbation. If your own value system finds masturbation an acceptable form of teenage sexuality, then it can offer your teens a way to withdraw, and at the same time deal with their building sexual urges without having intercourse.

Negative Approach: Avoidance

We have discussed how teens with low self-esteem and courage will often avoid life's problems rather than face them. Withdrawing into sexual activity, whether real or in fantasy, is one way for such teenagers to find some pleasure in their painful lives. Such teens may begin masturbating several times a day as they seek to escape into a world of sexual pleasure. Whatever your view about

masturbation, it is clear that a problem exists when it becomes a method of avoiding reality.

Goal #5: Sexuality as a Path to Challenge

Positive Approach: Reasonable Risk Taking

All but the most prudish of parents recognize that *some* sexual experimentation is going to occur during the teen years. For some teens, a first kiss may be the most exciting experience of the year. Others will go on to petting, some to intercourse. In addition, since sexuality includes the emotional aspects of the relationship as well as the physical, the challenge of learning how to risk being with others in an intimate relationship is important for the teen to deal with.

Of course, what is "reasonable" risk taking will depend on your own value system. Is kissing okay, but petting going too far? We'll explore the value aspects of sexuality more fully in the next chapter.

Negative Approach: Thrill Seeking

Remembering that the teen years are the period when most people want the most challenge in their lives, the discouraged teen may look for the cheap thrill as a means of approaching this goal. Sex, like drugs, offers these teens easy access to such excitement.

The challenge for parents is to teach teens that using sex as a contest or conquest, is disrespectful of the other person, and of oneself.

Traditionally, boys have been more tuned in to the goal of challenge, just as girls have been more interested in the goal of contact. Although this has begun to even out in recent years, boys are still more often the aggressors when it comes to the challenge of sex. The thrill of the hunt that was present for our primitive ancestors can still be seen played out in adult singles bars and in the lunchrooms of American high schools. The challenge for parents is to teach our sons and daughters that thrill seeking is a destructive path to challenge, and that using sex as a contest or conquest is disrespectful of the other person, and of oneself.

Chapter 12

The Parent as Sex Educator

The skills you learned earlier in this program can be used effectively to influence your teen towards positive sexual values and behavior. You can use these skills to accomplish four important tasks as a parent:

■ Provide your teen with accurate information about sexuality.
■ Talk with your teen about values regarding sexual behavior.
■ Become an "askable" parent.
■ Set limits regarding behavior.

Provide Your Teen With Accurate Information About Sexuality

Let's see how much you already know about sexuality. Can you identify these four influential sex educators? Kinsey, Masters and Johnson, and Ramsey. You may know something about the first three, but I doubt that you have the faintest idea who Ramsey was. That's because you didn't grow up in our neighborhood. Ramsey was the kid next door who was the biggest sex educator on the block. He taught me everything there was to know about sex, and he managed to get about 20 percent of it right (or so I found out years later).

If you are not teaching your teens about sexuality, then you can be sure that someone else is.

If you are not teaching your teens about sexuality, then you can be sure that someone else is. It may be more comfortable for you to let the Ramsy's of the world do the job for you, but the information is not going to be accurate. In these days when sex can be fatal, that's a risk you can no longer take. If you are fortunate enough to have a sex education program in your child's school, then get a copy of the material and reinforce it at home. Of course, you will also want to make sure the values are consistent with your own, but in this section we are stressing the importance of teaching the facts. Some of the facts that you will want to cover are:

■ The reproductive process (from A to Z; don't assume they already know; check it out). Pay special attention to correcting some of the common myths teens have about reproduction. For example:

   Myth: You can't get pregnant the first time you have intercourse.

   Myth: You can't get pregnant standing up.

■ Birth control. Whether you believe in abstinence, natural family planning or any of the conventional birth control methods available from condoms to the sponge, it is important that your teens be knowledgeable about the risks and benefits of each. Remember, they may not choose your values. In spite of all your best parenting efforts, they may decide to try sexual intercourse for themselves. It is senseless to compound a mistake like this by getting pregnant. The health and social risks of teen pregnancy are too great. Again, search and destroy the myths:

Myth: Douching after intercourse (with a soft drink) will prevent pregnancy.

Myth: You can't get pregnant if the male withdraws "in time."

■ Sexually Transmitted Disease (STD). The single greatest risk facing sexually active teenagers today is AIDS. And the kicker is they don't even know it. Most teens seem to believe that if they aren't gay, then AIDS isn't a problem. What we know, of course, is that AIDS has found its way into the heterosexual community, and that everyone is at risk. Of course your teens should also know about herpes, gonorrhea, syphilis, chlamydia, venereal warts and other sexually transmitted diseases.

Myth: Only gays get AIDS.

Myth: Penicillin will cure anything I get. (Penicillin only cures certain types of disease; AIDS and herpes are incurable.)

Active Parenting skills to use:

■ A blend of communication skills.

To become an effective sex educator for your teens and preteens, you will need to:

a. Get the facts. There are plenty of excellent books that will update you on the information you need. Spend some time going through one or more of these.

b. Sit down with your teens and preteens (one at a time if you have more than one; two or more can't seem to keep from laughing) and talk with them about one of the subjects you want to cover. A simple invitation will do:

"Honey, I've been wanting to talk with you about something for some time. How about tonight after dinner?" When you sit down after dinner, you might begin with a non-personal topic such as:

"You've probably heard a lot about AIDS on TV lately. I thought we should talk about it ourselves." Once you begin a discussion about sexuality on any topic, you can easily move into other topics. You may also want to find an appropriate book written for teens, and buy it for them. Be sure to read it yourself, and then be even more sure to discuss it with them after they have read it. (Don't cop out by expecting the book to do it all; your discussion will clarify misconceptions and underscore key points.)

Talk with Your Teen about Values Regarding Sexual Behavior

What do you want for your teens?

Your role is that of a consultant when it comes to teaching values.

I said earlier that this chapter will not tell you what values you ought to want for your teens. Sexuality and love are probably the most complex human experiences that we as parents have to deal with. Most of us have not thoroughly sorted out these issues for ourselves, and there is no uniform code of behavior or values in today's society. For you to be effective at communicating your own values to your teens, it will help if you take some time to clarify what you believe for yourself. If you are married, talk this over with your partner. You may find that you don't agree on everything. This is not a problem, because your teen is unlikely to agree with either of you 100 percent anyway. Remember, your role is that of a consultant when it comes to teaching values. You can't force them on your teen. He or she will ultimately choose a value system that seems right.

Some of the types of questions that you may want to think about are:

- What is the purpose of sexuality? Is it just to procreate? Is it also a means of expressing love? Is it also a means for achieving pleasure?

  _____

  _____

- Is it okay to enjoy sex without love? Without marriage?

  _____

  _____

- What do you believe about fidelity? Is extramarital sex wrong?

  _____

  _____

- What do you believe about birth control? Is abortion an acceptable form of birth control? Under what circumstances is abortion acceptable?

  _____

  _____

- What responsibility does a person have for his or her sexual partner? Is seduction okay? What do you believe about date rape?

  _____

  _____

- What do you believe about homosexuality? Do you believe it is an illness, a sin, a lifestyle choice, or just another way of being? If you found out that your teen was gay, would you have the courage to still be a loving parent?

  _____

  _____

- Is masturbation an acceptable way to let off sexual steam? If so, how much is too much? If not, why not? And what's the alternative?

  _____

  _____

Once you have clarified your own values, you will be in a more powerful position to influence your teens. Let's look at how to use your Active Parenting skills in this regard.

Active Parenting skills to use:

- **Mutual respect.** Your teen is entitled to his or her own opinions and should not be put down for believing differently from you. Your greatest task is to keep the lines of communication open between you, and you can't do this if you blame, shame or otherwise speak disrespectfully.

- **Avoid communication blocks.** Each of the communication blocks discussed in Session IV is a surefire way not only to end the conversation, but to motivate the child to rebel against your values as well. For example, consider the communication block "commanding." All teens want power, and the power to choose their own values is important to them. After all, one of their main tasks is to develop a philosophy of life. If you command your teen to believe a certain way, then the only way for her to feel that she has power over her beliefs is to believe the opposite!

- **Listen for feelings; consider their thoughts.**

Your greatest task is to keep the lines of communication open.

The ability to see the world through your teen's eyes and appreciate his feelings about things will pay rich dividends in any discussion of sexual values.

"It sounds like you felt embarrassed when all the guys were talking about how far they got on their dates, and you weren't trying to get your date into bed anyway."

"I guess you're saying that you think Dad and I make too big of a deal out of sex, that you believe that it's just another thing two people can do together to have a good time."

Encourage them

The systematic use of encouragement can help lead teens in the direction we would like them to go.

The systematic use of encouragement can help lead teens in the direction we would like them to go. For example, if you would like your teenage son to learn to treat women respectfully, catch him being respectful, and make a positive comment:

"Son, I couldn't help overhearing you talking to Brad in the kitchen tonight. I was walking through and heard you say that you didn't think referring to a girl in 10th grade as 'an easy piece' was a nice thing to say. I just wanted to tell you that I was proud of you."

To help your teens develop a positive value system about sexuality, you can do some other things as well:

■ **Set a positive example.** Just as with alcohol and other drugs, what you do is more important than what you say in the area of sexuality as well. If what you say you value is different from what your teens see you doing, then your credibility is shot, and you will have lost most of your ability to influence them. Remember, the ability to influence another's values comes mostly from their willingness to respect you and therefore your opinion. Without that respect, your teens will not care what you think or do.

Talk with your teens about their beliefs and values about sex.

■ **Take time to talk about values.** Just as it's important to talk with your teens about the facts of sex, it is at least as important to talk with them about their beliefs and values about sex. Because such values are more personal, they will need a high degree of trust in you before they will share freely. As was said earier, they must feel that you will respect their opinions, even if you disagree, and not judge or speak to them harshly if they open up.

It may help you restrain the natural tendency to judge others' values negatively by remembering that teens often try on values the way they do new clothes. Both change often. Both are sometimes tried on for the shock value. Both are usually outgrown. By staying low-key and nonjudgmental, you may one day find that you have been more of an influence than it seemed at the time.

On the other hand, if you blow up, or condemn their tried-on values, you may force them to solidify a position they would have liked to give up. I often tell rebellious teenagers that one of the most difficult things for them to do when they have an overbearing parent is to do what they really want to do, when it's also what the parent wants them to do. Don't make it difficult for your teens to accept *your* beliefs, by putting down *their* beliefs. Instead, you can disagree respectfully, and calmly state your own opinion. Once again, this works best with palms up and an "I don't know what you'll decide" attitude. For example:

Don't make it difficult for your teens to accept your beliefs, by putting down their beliefs.

"I respect your right to think of sex as just another way for people to enjoy each other, and I don't know what you will ultimately decide about that. My own opinion, however, is that sex *can be* something very special, if it's saved for a special time and place, with a special person. Sure, it can be just another recreational activity, and I know that can be fun. But you pay a price for treating it cheaply. That price is that you may never know how really great it can be when it's used only as an expression of love and commitment."

The soft-sell approach used in the above example will give this teen something to think about. His dad has not forced a confrontation, and so the door is left

open for the teen to accept the parent's view as his own at a later time. His tone is caring rather than judgmental, and he has appealed to his son's sense of reason, rather than his own authority.

You will find that there are many opportunities to begin a discussion about sexual values. For example, your talk about the facts of sex can easily lead into a discussion of values. Because the facts are not personal, it is usually easier to begin there, then bring up questions of values. You can also use TV shows, movies and news items to make the bridge into such discussions. Just find something in the story or plot that has to do with sexuality, and turn it into a question. For example:

Your talk about the facts of sex can easily lead into a discussion of values.

"I saw something on a TV movie last night that I wanted your opinion about. This guy and girl meet in a bar and get pretty drunk. They go home together and have sex, but they are either too drunk or just don't care because they don't use birth control. She gets pregnant. He says it's not his fault because he was drunk, and besides, 'It's the woman's job to take care of protection.' What do you think?"

When Talking About Values

- ■ Show respect.
- ■ Avoid communication blocks.
- ■ Listen to thoughts and feelings.
- ■ Come from caring, not judgment.
- ■ Come from reason, not authority.

Become an "Askable" Parent

One of the goals of all the communication skills we have been talking about is for you to become the type of parent that your teens will feel comfortable approaching when a conflict or problem arises. We call this being an "askable" parent because your teens "ask" you for your opinion or advice.

Active Parenting skills to use:

Mutual respect
Avoiding communication blocks
Encouragement
Active communication
Active problem solving

The first three of these skills will help you establish the trust that your relationship needs if your teens are to ask you about uncomfortable issues. Active communication and problem solving will enable you to help them find solutions to tough adolescent problems. Remember, when they own the problem, your job is to offer support, not discipline. Part of this support can be to help them roleplay how they might handle difficult situations such as the following:

- Your boyfriend tells you to prove that you really love him by going all the way. What do you do?

- You don't have a date for the big dance, and it's only two days away. There's a guy you like who still doesn't have a date either. What do you do?

- The other guys find out that you're a virgin and begin calling you names. What do you do?

Set Limits Regarding Behavior

Having less time to resist temptation makes it easier for them to maintain the values they have chosen.

Did you ever have that famous argument when you were a teenager? The one in which your parents wanted you home by a certain time, and you protested that they didn't trust you. Then you played your trump card and said defiantly, "Besides, there is nothing that could happen after midnight that I couldn't do before midnight if I wanted to."

The logic behind this argument is half right. Teens certainly can act out sexually before their curfew. We certainly cannot monitor their behavior 100 percent. However, sexuality is only partially a matter of which values the teens have chosen. The other half is how well they can stand up to the pressures from peers and their own sexual desires. Having less time to resist temptation makes it easier for them to maintain the values they have chosen. As with preventing

alcohol and drug use, monitoring their activities and providing adult supervision where possible is important.

Active Parenting skills to use:

Problem prevention
Logical consequences
Active problem solving
Encouragement

Involve teens in planning their own rules and limits.

Rather than laying down the law with teens, we have stressed the importance of involving them in planning their own rules and limits. This participation gives them a means of influencing the decisions that affect their lives without having to resort to rebellion. Together, you can come up with guidelines for these and other situations:

■ Establish and enforce a regular curfew.

When possible, meet with other parents in the community to establish some consistency. Logical consequences can be used to discipline curfew violations. Greater freedom in other areas can be used to encourage compliance with the curfews. Obviously, you will need to be up when they come home to monitor this. In addition, late night talks can be great opportunities to reinforce values and handle problems that may have occurred during the evening.

■ Know where your teens are.

Unless you are monitoring an out-of-control teen, you will not need to know where your teens are 100 percent of the time. This is unrealistic for you, and unfair to responsible teens. (An out-of-control teen has demonstrated an inability to monitor himself, and may need to be met after school by an adult for total supervision, at least until he has regained some trust.) You will want to know where your teens are for extended periods of time — for example, after school, when they are out in the evening, and on weekends. Arranging for them to call you when plans change is also a help.

■ Make sure parties and overnights are supervised by a responsible adult.

Beer blasts at somebody's cabin in the woods or overnight stays at someone's home when the parents are out of town invite trouble. Again, the more opportunity for temptation, the greater the risk of a mistake. Be aware that even basically responsible teens will sometimes be led into fabricating a situation, for example, telling parents they will be at a supervised party, then taking off with a group to an unsupervised place. For this reason, calling ahead to check out the arrangements with the supervising adult is a good idea.

A Code of Sexual Conduct

The culmination of your teen's thinking about sexual values might be a "value system" or "code of behavior" that he or she can live by. You can talk with your teens about such a code, and perhaps share the following as an example. You and your teens might add or delete from this as you see fit.

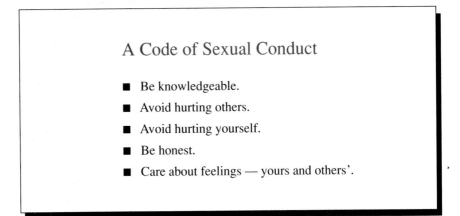

A Code of Sexual Conduct

- Be knowledgeable.
- Avoid hurting others.
- Avoid hurting yourself.
- Be honest.
- Care about feelings — yours and others'.

Giving Accurate Information

As you plan to talk with your teen about the facts of sexuality, use this guidesheet to help.

What topics will you want to discuss with your teen? (check and add)

❑ Reproduction
❑ Birth control
❑ AIDS
❑ Other sexually transmitted diseases

_____

_____

How will you expand your own knowledge of these topics?

❑ Buy a book
❑ Check a book out of the library
❑ See if my teen's school has a sex ed program,
  and ask to see their materials
❑ Talk to someone in the medical field

_____

_____

Remembering that talking regularly about sex is better than trying to cover everything at once, when will you have your *first* talk?

Afterwards...

What went well with your talk? _____

What will you do differently for your next talk?_____

When will your next talk be?_____

Talking to Your Teens About Values

Remembering that teens will ultimately choose their own values, think about how you can encourage them to make healthy choices.

To begin with, look back to page 178 and your beliefs about these questions:

What is the purpose of sexuality? (Is it only to procreate? Is it also a means of expressing love? Is it also a means of achieving pleasure?)

_____

What do you think about enjoying sex without marriage? Without love?

_____

What do you believe about fidelity? Is extramarital sex wrong?

_____

What do you believe about birth control? Is abortion an acceptable form of birth control? Under what circumstances, if any, is abortion acceptable?

_____

What responsibility does a person have for his or her sexual partner? Is seduction okay? What do you think about date rape?

_____

What do you believe about homosexuality? (Do you think it is an illness, a sin, a lifestyle choice, or just another way of being?) If you found out that your teenager was gay, would you still have the courage to be a loving parent?

_____

Is masturbation an acceptable way to let off sexual steam? If so, how much is too much? If not, why not? And what's the alternative?

_____

THEN YOU TALK TO YOUR TEENS ABOUT VALUES

Plan to spend some time talking with your teen about these values. Then check the guidelines you were able to follow. Did you...

- ❑ Talk respectfully
- ❑ Avoid communication blocks
- ❑ Listen for thoughts and feelings
- ❑ Come from caring, not judgment
- ❑ Come from reason, not authority

What will you do differently next time?

_____

Setting Limits on Behavior

What reasonable limits have you set for your teens regarding:

■ Curfew?

    weeknight_____

    weekend _____

    Are you awake when they come home?_____

■ Where they go?

    Do you know where they are?_____

    Do you check out the adult supervision with the
    adult in charge of parties and overnights?_____

■ Having opposite sex company over?

    Do you have a rule about leaving bedroom doors open?_____

■ What other limits have you set?_____

■ Do you have logical consequences in place for rule violations?_____

What will you do differently in the future?

_____

_____

_____

_____

_____

Letting Go

In the beginning of this program, we stated that the purpose of parenting is protecting and preparing our children and teens to survive and to thrive in the kind of society in which they will live. The idea of preparing our teens for a life independent of us is essential to active parenting. In fact, as important a job as parenting is to the future of our society, it is also one of the few jobs the purpose of which is to work oneself out of a job!

The most difficult task for any teenager is to break away from his or her parents...and then return as a fellow adult.

Someone once suggested that the most difficult task for any teenager is to break away from his or her parents...and then return as a fellow adult. Those families who have made this transition effectively know what a joy adult children can be. The skills presented in this program can set the stage for such a passage. But it will take one more thing: A willingness by you to let go.

I opened this program with a poem about courage and fear, because courage is the essential quality that a teen needs in order to make positive life choices. I think it fitting to close with another poem about courage — the courage it often takes for a parent to let go. We can help our teens build their ships, but if we try to tell them where to steer as they pull out of the harbor, we all end up gasping for air. If you can give this poem to your teen on the day that he or she leaves home, then you will have given the greatest message of en-couragement that I know.

I wish you well with your parenting. It's the most important job around, and you who take it seriously enough to spend time reading books like this hold the best hope for our collective future.

A Final Gift: Letting Go
(To a teen leaving home)

Boats in the harbor are safe near shore
Far from the unknown sea,
But just as boats were made for more,
It's the same with you and me.

Those who would anchor their teens with a stone
In hopes of preventing a wreck,
Find that their fears are never undone
And the stone ends up weighting *both* necks.

So I give to you a port called home
Where your ship was built so strong,
And if you need to harbor here,
You know that you belong.

And I give to you the maps you'll need
That you may set the course
For places that I'll never see,
So go without remorse.

Tilting your sails into the wind
With hope, and vision and courage —
I kiss you once, then touch your chin
And wish you bon voyage!

- - Michael H. Popkin
1989

Active Parenting Publishers has additional resources to help parents with

Parenting Skills

Self-Esteem Development

&

Loss Education

For more information, write:

810-B Franklin Court
Marietta, GA 30067